THE UNIVERSITY OF CHICAGO

TORONTO'S CHANGING RETAIL COMPLEX

A STUDY IN GROWTH AND BLIGHT

DEPARTMENT OF GEOGRAPHY
RESEARCH PAPER NO. 104

By

JAMES W. SIMMONS

University of Western Ontario

CHICAGO · ILLINOIS
1966

Library of Congress Catalog Card Number: 66-18572

PREFACE

As stated in the Work Program of the Metropolitan Toronto Urban Renewal Study, the purpose of the commercial study is "to provide an analysis of the location, extent, nature, and trends of commercial obsolescence in Metropolitan Toronto; to determine the effect of commercial blight upon residential conditions and to assist in the development of methods of renewal treatment and of alternative courses of renewal action." The pursuit of this purpose has inevitably involved various sidetrips to explore the nature of commercial structure, blight, and renewal. A detailed understanding of the retail and service sector is necessary in order to recognize blight, let alone suggest renewal action; and the terms blight and renewal each include many complex implications for commercial renewal.

I found the project to be doubly interesting: the growth and diversity of Toronto make it a fascinating study area, but more important has been the stimulation from working with my associates in this project. Mr. Samuel Cullers, Director of the Urban Renewal Study, and his staff have been invariably helpful. The imaginative and conscientious field work by Alan Baker and Larry Bourne made the data a pleasure to work with. Robert Murdie was most cooperative in providing the material from his special census analysis; and Brian Berry, of course, tied the whole program together with a constant stream of ideas. Eli Comay and Bert Elwood made very useful comments on the draft. Finally, I must thank Bob Grainger for his work on the calculator and, especially, my wife Harriet for her typing, calculating, key-punching, and proofreading.

The results gathered in this study represent the distillation of a large amount of data. Although limitations of time and money prevent the publication of much of this background information, it will be kept on file by the Metropolitan Toronto Planning Board for use by any interested parties.

TABLE OF CONTENTS

LIST OF TABLES

vii

LIST OF ILLUSTRATIONS

CHAPTER I

THE PROBLEM: COMMERCIAL BLIGHT IN TORONTO

The twenty thousand stores in the Metropolitan Toronto Planning Area
reach into almost every block. Since they seek easy access to passers-by they
are usually the most visible part of a neighborhood, dominating their sur-
roundings and shaping the image of the area. Run-down commercial areas with
vacant, uncared-for stores or dilapidated buildings quickly create an aura of
blight even in otherwise successful districts. Yet commercial blight is a complex phenomenon which may occur in almost any part of the metropolis. It is
particularly serious during this period of rapid growth and innovation, when
the commercial facilities of a wide area are threatened by various forms of
obsolescence. In this study we shall identify areas of blight, investigate the
causal factors behind them, and suggest programs to improve existing facilities
and to anticipate future problems.

The Definition of Commercial Blight

Trying to identify and delimit areas of commercial blight presents a
number of technical problems. The usual difficulties involved in gathering
statistics and making measurements and classifications are complicated by the
many different aspects of commercial blight. Blight is a term which has been
used to describe symptoms, causes, or remedies, and in the case of retail and
service areas has been applied to such disparate phenomena as tumble-down
buildings, surplus commercial space, or the noise and gaudiness of neon-lit
ribbon retailing.[1]

---

[1]A quick survey of the literature reveals a variety of interpretations
of the term blight. The Ontario Department of Municipal Affairs in its bro-
chure, Urban Renewal in Ontario (1964), says, "Blight is the deterioration of a
building, group of buildings, or a neighborhood. It may result from the age of
the building, from dilapidation, over-crowding, lack of community facilities,
obsolescence of building, faulty neighborhood layout, or the introduction of
new community facilities (such as an arterial road in the community area), or
from inadequate maintenance of buildings or community facilities." The same
department, in A Better Place to Live, says, "Three basic factors are involved
in the cause and, hence, in the control of blight, namely: (1) the individual
structure, (2) the environment, and (3) the residents themselves."
Coleman Woodbury (ed.), Urban Redevelopment: Problems and Practices
(University of Chicago Press, 1959), p. 11, uses blight as a general term, referring to an area or district and covering a wide range of conditions and
characteristics but especially characterized by substandardness and either
stagnation or deterioration.

In this study we shall differentiate between the blight phenomena them-selves such as vacant stores, decaying buildings, or congestion, and the factors which cause them such as age, competition, or technological change. It is also important to realize that there are many different forms of commercial blight, each of which should be defined independently and which may produce different spatial patterns. Given this diversity within the general definition, blight may be studied in either of two ways: by identifying blighted areas as districts which have a high concentration of all these various aspects of blight; or on a systematic basis, examining the city-wide distributions of the different types of blight. The former approach is appro-priate at the treatment stage, the latter is useful for analysis. Since this study is concerned with survey and analysis, and is dealing with widely dis-persed phenomena, the sectoral technique is used, stressing careful identification of the various forms of blight phenomena, each of which may then be traced backwards in time to the causal factors, or forward in time to possi-ble renewal procedures.

Earlier studies in other cities have specified at least four possible forms of commercial blight:

Physical blight occurs when the building occupied by a business has deteriorated.

Functional blight is obsolescence due to technological change which makes the location, size, or layout of the structure inefficient for its pre-sent commercial use.

Frictional blight occurs when the presence of nearby land uses has a harmful effect on the operation of commercial establishments.

Economic blight exists when there is an insufficient demand for existing retail facilities, creating a surplus of store space, or firms, or both.

Each of these forms of blight originates from a different cause and may occur independently. Yet there may also be interdependence: physical blight may be a result of any of the other factors which lead to economic inefficiency and reduced maintenance; and certain areas, especially older parts of the city which are undergoing rapid changes in population, may suffer from the whole syndrome of blight conditions.

These four types of blight were taken into consideration when the study of commercial obsolescence and deterioration in Toronto was planned. A field survey obtained detailed information on store functions, groupings of stores, physical deterioration and vacancy rates throughout the Metropolitan Toronto Planning Area, and this material was supplemented by 1961 census material and detailed land use information gathered by the Metropolitan Toronto Planning

Board. Before discussing the commercial study in detail it is important to review the two major bodies of conceptual material which are united in this study: the general principles which underlie the commercial structure of major metropolitan areas, and the unique characteristics of the Toronto area which may modify these general relationships.

A Review of the Theory of Metropolitan Commercial Structure

The theoretical background of the Toronto study which influenced the working hypotheses, and the collection and analysis of data, is derived from a series of investigations of the commercial structure and blight of the Chicago Metropolitan area.[1] Contained within these studies are reviews of relevant investigations in other urban areas. From time to time we shall compare the Toronto results with these earlier studies. The findings prior to this study may be summarized as follows:

1. The commercial facilities of a city form a system, a set of inter-related elements which interact to create a recognizable structure. There is a consistent emergence of similar business types and commercial aggregations. The variety of aggregations is summarized in Figure 1 and consists of three complementary systems. The centres, planned and unplanned, form a hierarchy: large centres serve the specialized needs of the customers in the trade areas of many smaller centres, each centre providing the goods and services appro-priate for its level to most of the residents within its trading area. The specialized areas on the other hand are groupings of one or two business types which derive mutual benefit from their spatial association and serve the whole, or a large part, of the metropolitan area population.

Between these extremes are retail ribbons, characterized by the form of their spatial grouping. The traditional shopping street is really a variant of the smaller centre. The other forms of ribbons are more complex forms of

---

[1]Brian J. L. Berry, Commercial Structure and Commercial Blight (Department of Geography Research Paper No. 85; Chicago: University of Chicago, 1963); Brian J. L. Berry and Robert J. Tennant, Chicago Commercial Handbook (Department of Geography Research Paper No. 86; Chicago: University of Chicago, 1963); Barry J. Garner, The Theory of Tertiary Activity and the Internal Structure of Retail Nucleations (unpublished Ph.D. dissertation, Northwestern University, 1963); James W. Simmons, The Changing Pattern of Retail Location (Department of Geography Research Paper No. 93; Chicago: University of Chicago, 1964); and Brian J. L. Berry and Robert J. Tennant, Metropolitan Planning Guideline: Commercial Structure (Chicago: Northeastern Illinois Metropolitan Area Planning Commission, 1964).

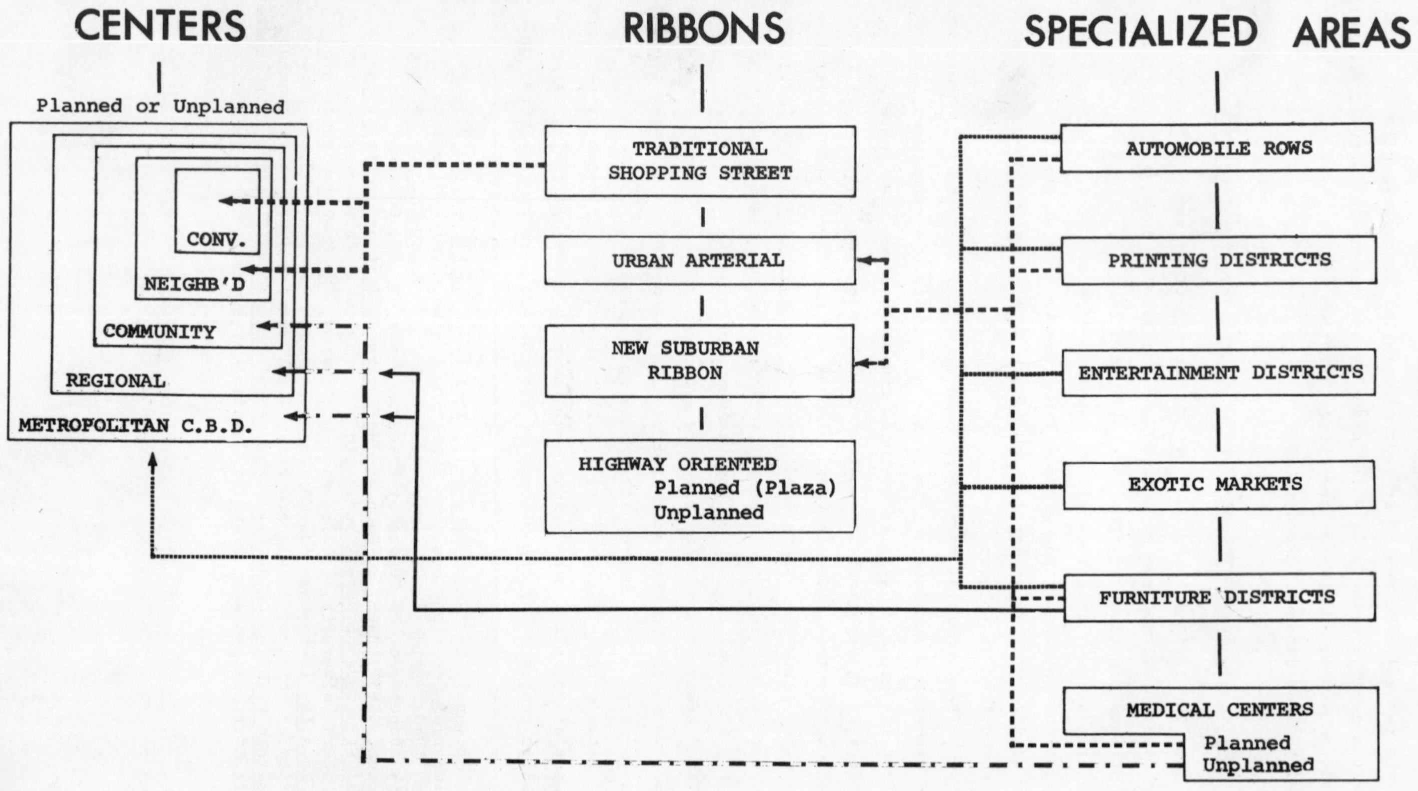

Fig. 1.—Commercial Structure

SPECIALIZED AREAS

AUTOMOBILE ROWS
PRINTING DISTRICTS
ENTERTAINMENT DISTRICTS
EXOTIC MARKETS
FURNITURE DISTRICTS
MEDICAL CENTERS
Planned
Unplanned

RIBBONS

TRADITIONAL SHOPPING STREET
URBAN ARTERIAL
NEW SUBURBAN RIBBON
HIGHWAY ORIENTED
Planned (Plaza)
Unplanned

CENTERS

Planned or Unplanned

CONV.
NEIGHB'D
COMMUNITY
REGIONAL
METROPOLITAN C.B.D.

specialized areas, whose trading areas are defined by the origin and desti-
nation of the major traffic arteries which they straddle.

2. The numbers and types of commercial facilities in an area are
determined by the size and characteristics of the population they serve. A
given population at a given income level can support only a certain number of
stores: the types of stores located in any area are determined by the
operating thresholds of the stores, their minimum supporting populations.
Moreover, different social areas demand different types of stores. Trade area
size, population, income level, sales, number of establishments, and number of
business types can be closely related by means of regression equations. Given
these relationships, changes in population or the social-economic class of an
area create strong pressures on the commercial facilities and lead to short-run
surpluses or deficiencies of retail space.

3. There are fundamental changes taking place in the commercial
structure itself in addition to the tremendous growth which has occurred in
most North American urban areas. Increased automobile ownership, greater
affluence, and widespread technological innovation have led to the doubling of
average store size, resulting in decreased number of stores in areas of stable
population. Planned centres with their radically different characteristics of
store "mix," location, and growth, dominate the newer parts of the city. Large
independent retailing units, supermarkets and discount houses, which are not
tied to the older patterns of commercial aggregation continue to develop.
Shifts in the consumer buying habits take place as incomes increase, fashions
change, and the demographic structure varies, altering the mix of stores.
There has been a shift in competition, which now occurs among centres rather
than among the stores of a given centre. The degree of change and its
apparent irreversibility are making large parts of the commercial structure
obsolete.

The Development of the Toronto Region[1]

Growth of the Urban Area

The typical commercial structure of a metropolitan area as presented
above is modified by unique characteristics of the urban region. Particularly
significant in Toronto has been the relatively recent growth into metropolitan
status. In Figure 2 growth curves for the three different urban regions, city,
Metro Toronto, and the planning area indicate that 50 per cent of the present
population has been added in the twenty-year period 1941-61, requiring rapid

---

[1]The Metropolitan Toronto Planning Board, Draft Official Plan of the
Metropolitan Planning Area (1959), includes a compact statement of the setting
and growth of the city.

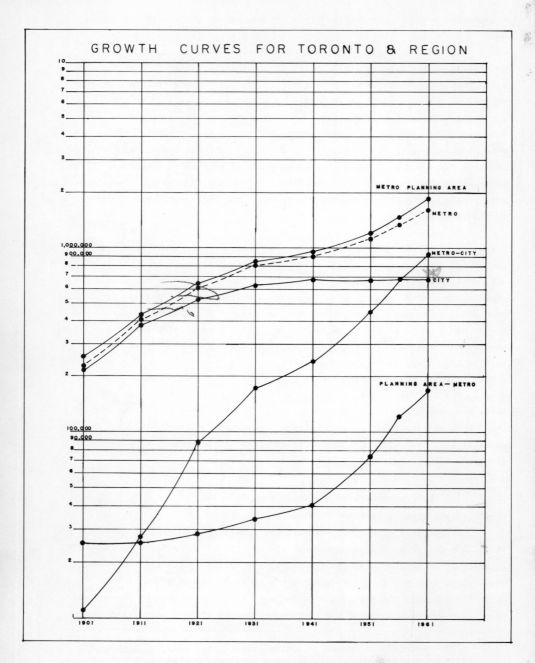

Fig. 2.--Growth Curves for Toronto and Region

adjustments in the previously existing structure. During this period the city has remained constant in population with growth concentrated in the outer areas (City: 0.0 per cent per year; Metro, 2.9 per cent per year; Planning Area, 3.2 per cent per year; all growth rates are compound).[1]

This rapid growth means that a large portion of the present commercial facilities are in modern structures and have been developed in equilibrium with present-day forces of mobility and consumer demand. However, those commercial areas which remain from an earlier era must adjust to a greatly changed city. This adjustment frequently results in functional blight. After the present commercial pattern is examined in Chapter II, these changes in the urban areas and in the nature of retailing will be studied in the third chapter in an effort to define the causes of commercial blight.

The city setting also has some implications for the commercial structure. The lakefront site has restricted growth to the northern sectors as shown in Figure 3, increasing the average distance of residential areas to the city centre and encouraging the development of outlying shopping centres. As the city grows the central business district is strongly skewed with respect to the population distribution and tends to move inland. The topography features a network of small river valleys or ravines particularly around the Don Valley to the east. Although the ravines had a strong barrier effect in the early development (note the difference between northwest and northeast in Figure 3), tending to isolate certain residential areas and create natural trade area boundaries, their effect is now reduced by the regional road grids which link all parts of the city creating the larger trade areas required for high order activities.

Although a regular arterial grid overlays this irregular topography, the most important development corridors followed the earlier routes in and out of the city: Dundas and Weston Road, Yonge, Kingston Road, and, later, Lakeshore Road. The patterns of development are reflected in variations of the commercial structure since each era has its own characteristic requirements of quantity, quality, and location of commercial facilities.

The Commercial Development

The commercial activities of the city were originally closely tied to the harbour, but as the city grew and hinterland connections by land emerged

---

[1]In referring to "Toronto" one may include at least three different areal units, shown most clearly in Figure 5. There is the city of Toronto itself, almost completely built by 1941 although changing internally since then; Metropolitan Toronto, the regional municipality; and the Planning Area of the Metropolitan Toronto Planning Board. The discussion will refer to each of these entities at various points.

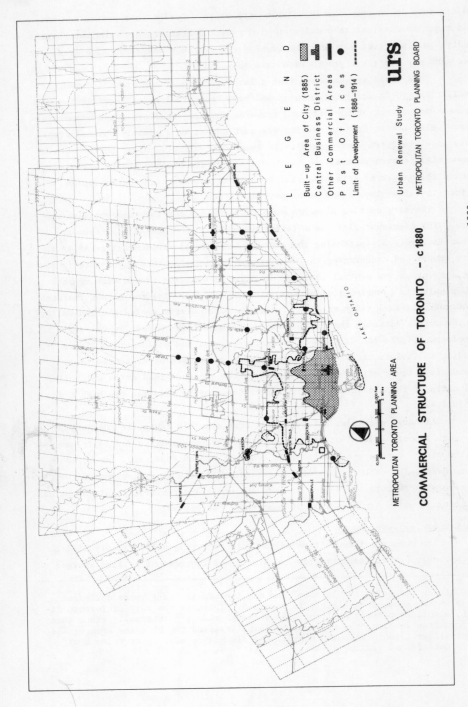

COMMERCIAL STRUCTURE OF TORONTO — c 1880

METROPOLITAN TORONTO PLANNING AREA

Urban Renewal Study

METROPOLITAN TORONTO PLANNING BOARD

L E G E N D

Built-up Area of City (1885)
Central Business District
Other Commercial Areas
Post Offices
Limit of Development (1886-1914)

Fig. 3.—Commercial Structure of Toronto—c1880

they expanded inland. The original core near Front and Church moved northwest to Yonge and King with the latter the main commercial artery for much of the late nineteenth century. Yonge Street has since taken over with two major commercial foci, the older core at Queen anchored by Eaton's and Simpson's department stores, and a growing fashion area at Bloor and Yonge.[1]

The central area dominated the built-up extent of the city until late in the nineteenth century. Beyond the urbanized area, though, were numerous small towns and villages which have since been integrated into Metropolitan Toronto (Figure 3).[2] Only one or two were exclusively residential suburbs, and the majority provided commercial facilities for their surrounding areas. They are important because their older, now obsolete, commercial structures show up on some of the blight distribution maps. As the city expanded rapidly in the period 1886 to 1915, these small centres were swallowed up and the present-day pattern of unplanned centres began to emerge.

Although the central area is still growing [from 2193 to 2479 stores and $482,000,000 to $538,000,000 sales (1951 dollars), 1951 to 1961] it is decreasing in relative importance in the Metro Toronto retailing structure. In 1951 it included 13.8 per cent of the stores, 34.3 per cent of sales; by 1961 these ratios had declined to 11.9 per cent of stores and 23.6 per cent of sales. The sales figures indicate the rapid dispersion of the large, high-order retailers.

Overview of the Results

The commercial study, although designed to study a specific problem in a specific city, achieved some results which are of more general interest.

The commercial structure was identified in detail and confirmed the results of earlier studies. Three broad zones were identified within the system, which were dominated by unplanned centres, planned centres, and outlying

---

[1]The commercial facilities of the area are discussed in detail by George H. Zieber, Toronto's Central Business District (mimeographed), M.A. Thesis, University of Toronto, 1961; and the City of Toronto Planning Board, Downtown Toronto, Background Studies for the Plan (Technical Series, No. 1, 1963), and Plan for Downtown Toronto (1963). The twin commercial foci are characteristic of three other metropolitan areas with which I am familiar: Chicago, Boston, and New York.

[2]The map is derived from material in the Historical Atlas of the County of York (Toronto, 1878), augmented by various historical sources. Appearing soon after 1880 were Mt. Dennis at Eglinton and Weston Road, North Toronto on Yonge just north of Eglinton, and Mimico. Rae Corelli, The Toronto That Used to Be (Toronto Star, 1964), describes some of these suburbs around the turn of the century as they were being integrated into the city proper.

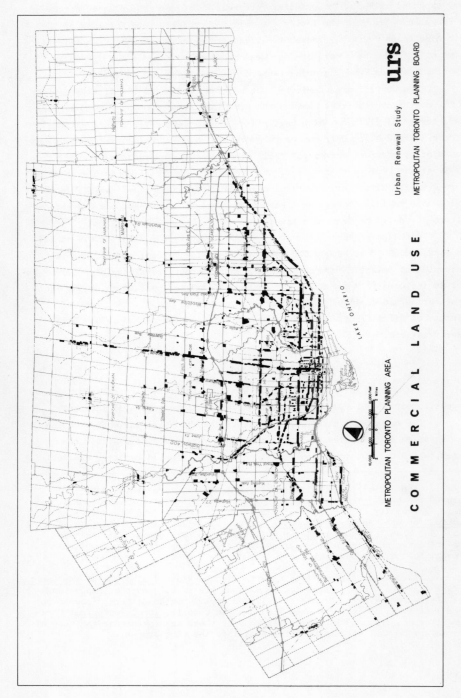

Fig. 4.—Commercial Land Use

U.R.

central places respectively, as one moves outward from the city centre. Various forms of retailing ribbons exist in new areas as well as old, together with a variety of specialized areas. When the relationships between the consumer and these retailing elements were explored detailed social characteristics of consumers were found to be useful in explaining commercial distributions.

The occurrence of blight in this system is quite complex. Each of the four types of blight posited earlier: physical, economic, functional, and frictional were found to occur independently. Functional blight is by far the most serious problem, with a wide area of the city threatened by several kinds of obsolescence. There are long-run changes in the parameters of relationships linking retail facilities and consumers as the sales and stores generated by a given population varies, and the entire retail system tends to shift outwards from the city centre. The stores of the older area are too small or have inadequate facilities for today's retailing. Many are now badly located since their customers have become highly mobile and the patterns of movement in the city have altered. Finally, new types of retail outlets are emerging in response to changing consumer needs so that some of the older business types are no longer needed; the product they sell or the services which accompany it are no longer what the buyer wants.

Urban renewal for problems such as these is a matter of adjustment--encouraging these changes to take place as painlessly as possible. The size, complexity, and rapidity of change in the commercial structure indicate the need for continuing programs of investigation to provide the necessary feedback of information for good planning and viable renewal decisions.

CHAPTER II

THE COMMERCIAL STRUCTURE OF TORONTO

In order to pinpoint the various causes of blighted commercial areas,
it was first necessary to describe the present structure of retail and service
activity in Toronto. Several sources of data were used to identify and locate
the various elements of the systems and to define their interaction. The
Dominion Bureau of Statistics provided information on retail and service activity by census tract for 1951 and 1961;[1] the Metropolitan Toronto planning
board had data on land use for 1964 as well as numerous compilations of data on
commercial activities; and the City of Toronto had data on land use and land
value by establishment.

Since it was necessary to obtain more detailed information about the
retailing structure, especially the various measures of blight, a detailed
field study was made to augment the other material. The field study also gave
the investigators an opportunity to inspect the Toronto commercial structure at
first-hand, providing insights into additional variables required for the
analysis.

The Inventory of Commercial Facilities

The field work was done in the period June to September, 1964, by two
observers working on foot and by car. Initial information concerning the location of commercial land use was obtained from maps compiled by the Metropolitan
Toronto Planning Board in the spring of 1964. More detailed information was
sought about:

1. The function and location of each retailing and service establishment in the planning region.

2. Significant patterns of grouping of these establishments including
planned centres, unplanned centres, and retail or service specialty areas.

3. The location of commercial buildings that were vacant, deteriorated,
converted to non-commercial uses, or newly constructed but not yet ready for
occupancy.

---

[1]Dominion Bureau of Statistics, Selected Distribution Statistics by
Census Tract for 14 Canadian Cities (Ottawa, 1954); Retail Trade, Metropolitan
Areas by Census Tracts and Service Trade, Metropolitan Areas by Census Tracts
(Ottawa, 1964).

The Study Area.--The study covered the Metropolitan Toronto Planning Area, which includes three distinct zones of commercial development (Figure 5): the older part of the city, served by unplanned shopping areas; the rapidly growing periphery of the city containing a proliferation of planned centres; and, further out, a still undeveloped region containing a number of older centres which serve as central places for the surrounding rural areas.

The central area (defined for the purpose of this study as census tracts 69 through 76 inclusive and tract 96) was excluded because the special nature and problems of this area require an analysis beyond the scope and resources of this study. The unique problems of obsolescence and blight in this area, although certainly a part of the overall picture, require such studies to be placed within the context of the changing role of the central business district within the metropolitan area.

The field crew surveyed all the main arterial streets and concession roads throughout the study area and all other commercial areas which had at least four commercial establishments grouped together, "grouped" meaning that there were no significant distances (of the order of a block) between stores which would discourage pedestrian traffic between them. Exceptions to this requirement were made to include all major retailing establishments such as discount stores or furniture stores.

The Classification of Types of Business.--The exact nature of the business activity in a retail or service establishment was defined in the field according to a classification established especially for the study. The Standard Industrial Classification of the Dominion Bureau of Statistics,[1] a three digit classification, was expanded to a four digit system, following the pattern of the United States' Bureau of the Budget[2] to provide the more exact identification of retail and service businesses which the Chicago experience had shown to be necessary. For instance, D. B. S. category 631 (Food Stores) was broken down into 6310 (Supermarkets), 6311 (Bake Shops), etc. Appendix A contains a replica of the classification sheet and illustrates the technique of field mapping.

The field sheets differentiated between ground floor and upper floor land uses and noted other information such as vacant commercial structures, new construction, conversions of commercial structures to other uses and adjacent

---

[1]Canada, Dominion Bureau of Statistics, Standard Industrial Classification Manual (Ottawa: Queen's Printer, 1960).

[2]United States, Bureau of the Budget, Standard Industrial Classification Manual (Washington: Government Printing Office, 1957).

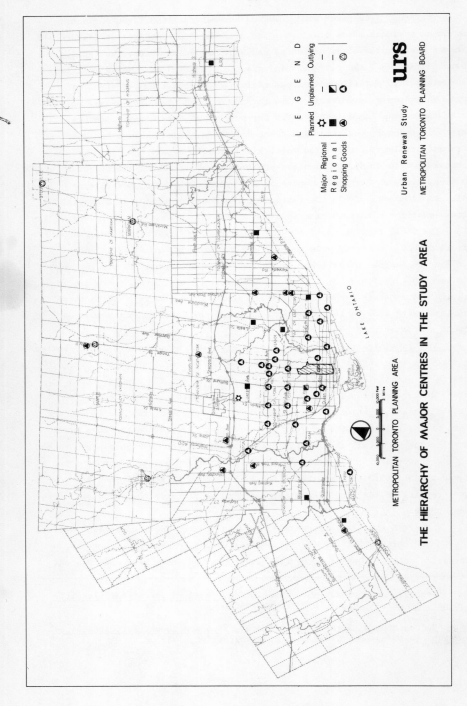

Fig. 5.—The Hierarchy of Major Centres in the Study Area

land use. The information on the field sheets also indicated planned strips,
clusters of commercial establishments, unplanned centres and census tract boundaries. Planned centres were described on separate sheets.

Trade Area Data.--During the gathering of field data, efforts were made
to obtain information on trade areas using the home interview material of the
Metropolitan Toronto and Region Transportation Study. Had this been successful
we would have had valuable evidence concerning natural trading boundaries, the
relative importance of the various centres and the relationship of a centre to
its trade area, providing further insights into the hierarchy of centres. It
is suspected that unplanned centres completely dominate their trade areas,
whereas planned centres have larger trade areas which overlap one another. The
latter are more specialized and cater to certain income groups since the suburban consumers regularly visit a number of competing centres.

The Aggregation of Field Data

In order to assess this body of information it was necessary to classify it and group it into more manageable units. The categories of unplanned
and planned centres, commercial ribbons, and specialized areas were based on
the initial hypotheses concerning commercial structure. Table 1 summarizes the
distribution of retail and service stores among these different groupings.
Note that commercial land use is predominately a ground floor use; and that
given our criteria for defining centres, is predominately in ribbon and
scattered form. Planned shopping plazas now make up 12.6 per cent of the outlying commercial establishments. In order to make the headings on this table
more meaningful, the particular criteria adopted for this analysis and the
special circumstances or limiting factors which led to their development are
presented in the sections which follow.

Unplanned Centres

Older arterial streets within the city are lined with block after block
of commercial establishments, yet it is evident that certain parts of this
ribbon, generally the main intersections, have a wider selection of stores,
higher land values, and attract customers from a wider area.[1]

---

[1]Berry, Commercial Structure and Commercial Blight, p. 29. The internal
structure of unplanned centres has been examined in detail by Garner, The Theory
of Tertiary Activity and the Internal Structure of Retail Nucleation.

TABLE 1

DISTRIBUTION OF COMMERCIAL ESTABLISHMENTS BY TYPE OF AGGREGATION[a]

A. Numbers of Establishments

		Ground Floor	Upper Floor	Total
Centres		4997	1141	6138
	Unplanned	4091	993	5084
	Planned	906	148	1054
Ribbon, Scattered and Small Nucleations		14412	1995	16407
	Unplanned	13225	1747	14972
	Planned	1187	248	1435
Total		19409	3136	22545

B. Per Cent of Row Total

Centres		81.6	18.4	100
	Unplanned	80.5	19.5	100
	Planned	85.5	14.5	100
Ribbon, Scattered and Small Nucleations		87.8	12.2	100
	Unplanned	88.7	11.3	100
	Planned	81.2	18.8	100
Total		87.8	12.2	100

C. Per Cent of Column Total

Centres		25.6	36.3	27.0
	Unplanned	20.7	31.6	22.5
	Planned	4.9	4.7	4.5
Ribbon, Scattered and Small Nucleations		74.4	63.7	73.0
	Unplanned	67.8	54.0	64.9
	Planned	6.6	9.7	8.1
Total		100	100	100

[a]By comparison, the City of Chicago and its two neighboring counties, Cook and Dupage, contained almost 90,000 establishments of which 3.9 per cent were contained in centres (3.2 per cent and 0.7 per cent in unplanned and planned centres respectively) and the other 96.1 per cent in scattered and ribbon. The Chicago definition of unplanned centre was more severe, and planned centres were at an earlier stage of development.

Intersections upon which such activities focus can be recognized as business centres, yet the differences in land use inside and outside the boundaries of such centres are so subtle as to defy simple means of identification. Failure to define centres accurately leads to errors when comparing them.

The problem of defining a centre has two stages: first, of determining whether one exists, and second, of defining its limits. Earlier studies used land values to great advantage in identifying centres, setting a minimum land value as a requirement, for "centre" status, and charting the breakpoints in the land value profile across the centre as a guide to choosing boundaries. However, in Toronto, the data on the assessed value of land was available only for individual lots and presented an impossible data handling problem. Moreover, the variation in the ratio of assessment to real property values between districts within the Metropolitan Area precluded the use of assessment figures. The alternative for this part of the study was to define the centres in the field using a number of criteria which earlier studies had established as significant indicators of the presence of a centre:[1]

1. High order functions.--Business centres contain business types requiring access to a large number of customers. The presence of chain variety stores (6472), candy stores (6312), large supermarkets (6310), clothing stores (66--), other specialty shopping goods (69--), financial services (70--), and business services (86--) indicates a commercial centre.

2. Upper floor uses.--Centres often contain high order services on the second and higher floors of buildings.

3. Continuity of commercial uses.--The high land value at the core of the business centre creates pressures that tend to convert other land uses to commercial within the centre. Breaks in the continuity of commercial uses which indicate a break in the flow of pedestrian traffic help delimit a centre.

4. Absence of low order functions.--Certain business types which do not require the high access to customers indicate low-value, non-centre areas. These include service stations (6541), professional offices at the ground floor (80-- to 86--), beauty and barber shops (8721, 8722) and the like. If such uses are not entirely eliminated as one nears the heart of the business centre, they are greatly reduced in number. Since the unplanned centre is pedestrian oriented, the presence of functions serving the motorists (65-- or drive-ins) is another indicator of a non-centre area.

---

[1]The centres as defined in this study are shown in Figure 22, Appendix B.

    5. <u>Physical barriers</u> such as railroads, parks, ravines, etc., are
likely centre boundaries since they impede the continuous flow of pedestrian
traffic.

    Table 2 summarizes the information obtained for unplanned business
centres.[1] The number of ground floor business types in a centre ranges from
35 to 71 (mean of 50), and establishments from 63 to 207 (mean of 126). Only
one centre has a department store, generally an indicator of higher order
retailing. The lack of variation in the range of activities present is a
result, on the one hand, of the small size of the city during the period of
growth of unplanned centres (until 1950) which precluded the development of
regional centres. At the other end of the scale, our definition of business
centres was too rigorous to include the many small community and neighborhood
commercial concentrations.

    There is, however, considerable diversity among centres of similar size.
The upper floor establishments have been segregated since they are generally of
a service nature and do not attract customers to other stores in the centre.
Upper floor business activity is negligible for most centres except Yonge-
Eglinton and Yonge-St. Clair, both which have heavy concentrations of financial
and professional offices (7000-7099) and business services (8610-8699), indicating that they are performing office functions normally found in the central
business district. College-Clinton has a high concentration of food stores and
Weston a number of automobile oriented stores, although by and large the relative concentration of retail units is quite consistent.

    The hierarchy of centres was devised after consideration of all this
information and in conjunction with the data on planned centres (Table 3). It
is quite simple: twenty-eight centres at the shopping goods level and one
regional centre, the latter ranked higher because of the presence of a major
discount department store which attracts customers from throughout the city.

Each centre may be regarded as dominating its surrounding area, but in turn
subordinate to the central business district. Conceptually, the business
centre is important for the interaction of its component establishments and its
attraction or centrality for retailing, which led us to disregard the variation
in upper floor facilities for the purpose of establishing the hierarchy. Yet

-----

    [1]As a test of the above criteria some of the Toronto centres selected and
defined on this basis were evaluated against sa mples of land value measured by
assessment per front foot. The results indicated that the functional boundaries of a Toronto centre extend slightly beyond the land value break points so
that the results of analysis of these centres may not be comparable with other
studies although internally consistent within the Toronto area.

within the hierarchy the variations among individual centres may be used to
classify them for other purposes such as examining employment patterns or
traffic generations. Differences in blight characteristics or in the quality
of stores within the various business types exist as well, creating an impres-
sion of uniqueness and diversity which the purpose of our analysis has forced
us to disregard.

Planned Centres

The retail facilities of a large part of the metropolitan area are
dominated by planned shopping plazas. They are differentiated from the
unplanned centres by their integrated building design, lack of internal competition, unified management, and presence of large free parking areas. These
factors affect certain internal variables including the mix and size of stores
and the number of stores of each kind.[1]

Classification of the planned centres required the establishment of two
different limits: the separation of planned centres from planned strips, a
form of ribbon development with a number of stores sharing one building, but
with little interaction between them; and the identification of major centres
comparable to the scale of the unplanned centres.

In the first case, factors which indicate centres include the presence
of more than ten stores, a supermarket, off-street parking in significant quan-
tities, limited access from the street, and the presence of non-service business
types.

The larger centres were defined using the same criteria as for unplanned
centres but stressing the nature of the business types rather than number of
stores. There are marked differences in the business types found in planned
centres at different levels in the hierarchy, since larger centres do not necessarily contain the full range of lower order goods. A high order planned
centre will have a much higher proportion of its stores selling shopping goods
than its equivalent unplanned centre.

Table 3 summarizes data for the top three levels of centres which are
comparable in facilities to the unplanned centres: super regional, regional,
and shopping goods. Appendix B contains further data on 69 community and
neighborhood planned centres--the other two levels. The hierarchy of planned
centres is more complex than for unplanned centres, in part because planned
centres are found towards the outer edge of the built-up area where the central

---

[1]Simmons, The Changing Pattern of Retail Location, Chapter IV.

TABLE 2

MAJOR UNPLANNED SHOPPING CENTRES IN THE TORONTO AREA

Name	Code No.	Business Types	Ground Floor			Upper Floor	
			Est.	Per Cent Vacant	Per Cent Deteriorated	B.T.	Est.
Bloor-Bathurst	R 1	59	145	5.8	5.8	16	35
Yonge North	S 1	71	172	4.4	1.1	6	7
Bloor-Jane	S 2	64	207	2.8	0.5	14	30
Danforth-Pape	S 3	62	183	4.2	3.1	10	11
Yonge-Castlefield	S 4	61	144	2.0	4.1	12	25
Bayview	S 5	58	135	4.3	0.0	13	31
New Toronto	S 6	58	136	3.5	0.7	11	29
Bloor-Dovercourt	S 7	57	175	0.6	6.3	12	20
Bloor-Royal York	S 8	56	126	1.6	0.0	8	24
Dundas-Keele	S 9	55	156	6.0	3.6	15	29
Eglinton-Avenue Rd.	S 10	53	143	4.0	0.0	11	22
Queen-Bathurst	S 11	50	152	5.6	9.3	8	10
St. Clair-Dufferin	S 12	49	156	0.6	1.9	13	36
Queen-Lansdowne	S 13	49	155	3.1	8.1	6	6
Yonge-St. Clair	S 14	49	122	3.2	0.0	29	93
Parliament-Carlton	S 15	48	111	3.5	0.9	3	17
Weston	S 16	48	97	4.9	4.9	7	27
Mt. Pleasant	S 17	45	110	0.0	0.0	4	4
Eglinton-Dufferin	S 18	45	103	3.7	0.9	13	34
Gerrard-Coxwell	S 19	44	95	4.0	1.0	4	5
Queen-Broadview	S 20	44	91	5.5	6.6	2	2
Eglinton-Bathurst	S 21	43	93	4.1	0.0	15	41
Danforth-Woodbine	S 22	41	88	3.3	0.0	13	24
Kingston Road-Victoria Pk	S 23	40	103	5.6	0.0	6	10
Queen-Lee	S 24	40	102	10.5	4.4	3	6
Yonge-Eglinton	S 25	40	92	5.2	0.0	37	395
College-Clinton	S 26	39	122	2.4	2.4	9	21
Eglinton-Keele	S 27	39	77	5.2	0.0	7	10
St. Clair-Vaughan Rd.	S 28	35	63	6.0	0.0	15	30

TABLE 2--<u>Continued</u>

				Ground Floor Establishments						
Food	Gen.	Auto	Clothes	House-hold	Others	Finance	Comm. Serv.	Bus. Serv.	Pers. Serv.	Misc.
14	6	0	35	7	30	6	12	2	30	1
19	7	4	30	16	31	9	7	1	45	3
29	6	5	44	13	25	16	15	1	48	3
20	10	2	47	14	26	13	10	1	34	5
14	4	5	30	16	26	5	5	1	37	1
15	5	4	20	12	22	9	8	7	34	0
12	8	3	24	16	13	13	9	2	31	3
26	9	1	42	21	18	5	8	2	41	2
16	2	3	27	10	22	10	11	1	23	0
18	9	4	33	15	25	8	2	3	33	1
18	8	3	32	3	27	10	4	2	36	2
22	6	1	38	24	19	3	5	0	35	0
21	6	2	46	15	28	10	8	1	29	0
28	10	0	37	9	23	6	2	0	39	1
13	1	5	28	3	17	15	3	2	32	3
13	6	0	19	12	14	4	5	1	34	2
8	3	<u>10</u>	18	13	16	6	3	1	17	1
13	6	1	16	10	18	7	4	1	35	4
9	9	2	25	7	14	12	4	1	17	3
19	9	3	16	8	13	3	3	1	18	2
10	5	1	<u>12</u>	11	<u>15</u>	3	2	2	30	0
13	1	1	14	4	12	9	5	4	29	1
9	4	0	21	10	18	5	7	0	14	0
17	7	2	14	7	13	4	2	0	24	3
13	7	0	14	6	14	5	12	1	31	0
4	3	0	<u>5</u>	2	16	|26|	6	8	21	1
30	5	1	26	8	17	6	7	0	20	2
6	6	2	13	8	10	5	4	2	22	0
4	4	4	12	5	10	3	4	0	16	1

TABLE 3

MAJOR PLANNED SHOPPING CENTRES IN THE TORONTO AREA

Name	Code No.	Ground Floor			Upper Floor		Leading Functions	
		B.T.	Est.	Per Cent Vacant	B.T.	Est.	Dept. Stores	Chain Variety Stores
Yorkdale	SR 1	45	77	18.0[a]	0	0	2	1
Don Mills	R 1	52	89	0.0	0	0	1	1
Cloverdale	R 2	42	58	0.0	0	0	1	1
Ajax	R 3	39	58	3.3	12	15	Discount	
Shopper's World	R 4	37	54	0.0	0	0	1	1
Thorncliff Pk.	R 5	32	38	2.6	3	9	Discount	1
Cedarbrae	R 6	30	46	0.0	6	9	1	2
Dixie	R 7	29	40	0.0	5	11	Discount	
Lawrence	R 8	23	36	2.7	6	7	1	2
Northtown	S 1	34	47	0.0	7	8		3
Knobhill	S 2	32	46	0.0	5	6		2
Dufferin	S 3	32	45	6.3	3	3		2
Crang	S 4	32	44	2.2	8	11		
Richmond Heights	S 5	32	39	2.5	0	0		1
Golden Mile	S 6	31	43	0.0	11	14		2
Applewood Village	S 7	31	34	8.1	8	16		1
Parkway	S 8	26	36	2.7	10	15		2
Rexdale	S 9	26	35	0.0	7	9		1
Royal York	S 10	26	30	3.2	5	10		1
Eglinton Square	S 11	22	26	0.0	4	4	1	1

[a]Recently opened, new construction.

area is less dominant. Some centres are challenging the central business district in the variety of shopping goods. Figure 6 indicates the location of the
major centres.

Like the unplanned centres, there is some variation among planned
centres of the same level. Some differences are not observable from our data

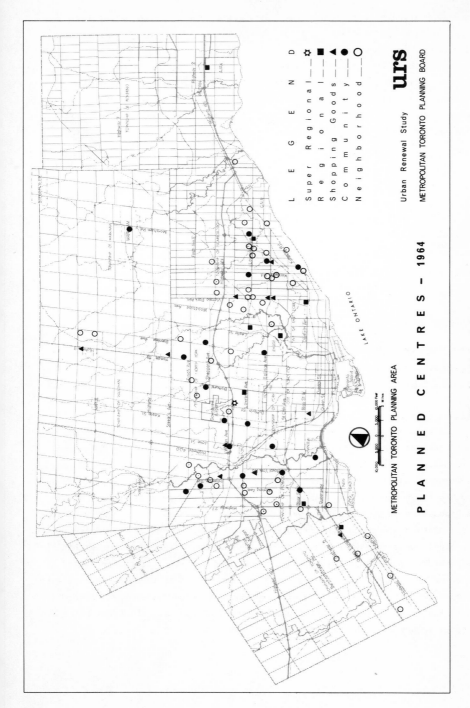

Fig. 6.--Planned Centres

⊄since they involve variations within the business type category, particularly the price and quality of goods, hence the sector of the population at
which the centre is aimed.

Another distinguishing feature is the presence of business and professional services in a number of shopping plazas, specifically Kenlinton,
Eastown, Agincourt, Bloordale, Flemingdon Park, Cliffcrest, Princess Plaza,
Bendale, and Crestview. The presence of these activities distorts the usual
relationships between establishments, business types, and trade area characteristics.

TABLE 4

THE HIERARCHY OF BUSINESS CENTRES

Level in Hierarchy	Unplanned	Planned	Characteristic Business Types
Super Regional	1 (central area)	1	2 or more department stores
Regional	1	8	1 department store and shopping goods
Shopping Goods	28	11	1 or 2 chain variety and shopping goods
Community	not defined	19	chain variety plus some shopping goods
Neighbourhood	not defined	60	supermarket

Outlying Centres

Table 5 presents the summary data for the six small central places
beyond the perimeter of planned centres. These centres originally served the
surrounding rural areas but their trade areas are slowly filling up with rural
non-farm and suburban residents. Nonetheless, their origins and roles differ
from the other types of centres and they are grouped separately in our study.
The boundaries of these centres were defined by the census tract limits of the
municipalities since any establishments within the town can be considered much
more highly aggregated than those outside. However, planned centres within
their borders are grouped with the other planned centres. At the upper end of
the scale the facilities of these towns are equivalent to those of the unplanned
business centres within the city although Markham drops below this standard.
They reflect the external central place pattern of the city which may be
expected to parallel the internal pattern.

TABLE 5

OUTLYING CENTRAL PLACES IN THE TORONTO AREA

		Ground Floor			Upper Floor	
		Business Types	Establish-ments	Per Cent Vacant	Business Types	Establish-ments
Port Credit	CT 406	64	163	5.2	19	39
Streetsville	CT 407	47	81	10.0	5	5
Woodbridge	CT 510	38	59	1.7	0	0
Richmond Hill	CT 502	58	116	7.2	8	20
Markham	CT 513	41	66	4.6	5	5
Stouffville	CT 514	45	73	2.1	0	0

Ribbon and Scattered Retailing[1]

The smaller unplanned retail nucleations, the planned centres smaller
than the shopping goods level, the various forms of ribbon retail aggregations,
the isolated stores, and the specialized shopping districts were lumped within
the general category of ribbon retailing. Problems of definition and functional classification of these aggregations make it very difficult to cate-
gorize them more precisely (except for the planned ribbons which consist of the
community and neighbourhood centres shown in Figure 7). However, some maps
have been prepared to indicate the general location patterns of the different
types of ribbon and scattered retailing without attempting exact measurement.
Figures 7 and 8, showing the various kinds of unplanned ribbons, were obtained
by examination of the field sheets. For mapping purposes a ribbon was required
to have a group of at least ten commercial establishments and each grouping was
arbitrarily categorized according to the predominant business types (see Table
6). The specialized commercial districts were cross-checked with the yellow
pages of the Toronto telephone directory.

The hierarchy of ribbon retailing: neighbourhood, urban arterial, and
shopping goods, roughly corresponds to the hierarchy of centres, but lacks the
internal structure within the grouping and the interaction between stores. The

---

[1]The term ribbon here includes all facilities outside of centres--in a
functional sense, all stores which do not have a high degree of customer interaction among them. Many planning studies define ribbon by location, i.e., a
continuously built-up commercial frontage of specified length. This limited
definition corresponds to the subset of ribbons mapped in Figure 7, but is
difficult to quantify.

TABLE 6

CHARACTERISTIC RIBBON RETAILING BUSINESS TYPES

RIBBON RETAILING

Neighbourhood	63--	Food
	6473	Variety
	6731	Hardware
	681	Drugs
	7021	Bank
	871 to	Personal
	8752	Services
Urban Arterial	6471	Discount Stores
	65--	Automobile Products
	67--	Hardware, Household Furniture, and Appliances
	7---	Financial Services
Shopping Goods	66--	Clothing and Shoes
	69--	Miscellaneous Retailing

SPECIALIZED COMMERCIAL DISTRICTS

Highway Oriented	6541	Service Stations
	8752-3	Restaurants
	8754-5	Hotels, Motels
Automobile Row	6561-2	New, Used Cars
	658-	Auto Repair
Medical Centres	681	Drug Stores
	821 to	Health
	8279	Services
Professional Offices	7---	Finance, Insurance, and Real Estate
	86--	Business Services
Furniture and Appliance	67--	

---

neighbourhood ribbon are often found in the centres of the blocks defined by the arterial grid. The urban arterial and shopping goods ribbons are found on the major traffic arteries, linking the unplanned centres. The major through streets in and out of the city--Yonge, Bathurst, Weston Road, Eglinton, St. Clair, Bloor-Danforth, College, Queen, Dundas, Lake Shore Road, and Kingston Road--are notable for their extensive commercial activity. In the outer parts of the city these ribbons co-exist with planned centres, the latter dominating in Scarborough, but the arterial ribbon more extensive in the western part of Metro (refer to Figure 6).

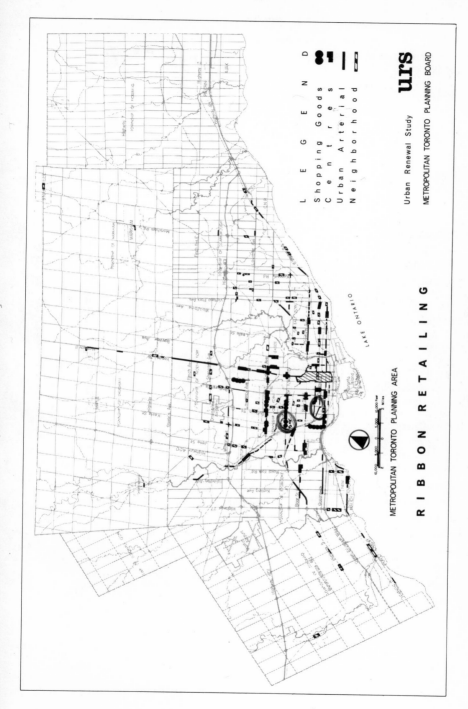

Fig. 7.--Ribbon Retailing

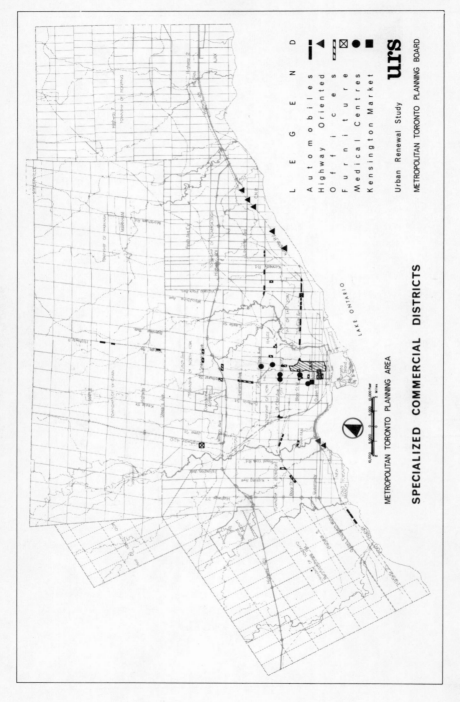

Fig. 8.--Specialized Commercial Districts

The distribution of the specialized commercial districts also shows some regularity. The periphery of the central business district, having access to the entire metropolitan area, has generated a number of these groupings: Kensington Market, the garment district, and a furniture-antique area. Also closely associated with the core of the city is a concentration of business and professional offices just north of the central business district in a high density upper-middle class residential area.

Kensington Market is a colourful concentration of ethnic specialty food stores (76 of a total of 113) and clothing stores, all extending into the streets, weather permitting. Just to the south of it is the garment district with business types 6671, 6691, women and children's wear; and 8699, unclassified business services. The area is interspersed and surrounded by blighted residential land use.

Automobile dealers are found in two main areas, east and west of the city, as are two highway-oriented ribbons which catch the major routes in and out of the city. These specialized areas which trade with a large segment of the metropolitan population will introduce a certain amount of inaccuracy into any attempt to explain commercial structures as a function of the characteristics of the local population.

Overview

At this point we may pause and take stock of the findings. The commercial structure of Toronto consists of a set of hierarchies of centres, unplanned in the older parts of the city, planned in the post-war areas, which satisfy the convenience and shopping needs of the immediately surrounding area up to a certain level of retail specialization. This level does not vary widely among the unplanned centres, which are all dominated by the central area, although some have added professional services which serve the whole metropolitan area. The hierarchy of planned centres is becoming more and more complex as the city grows, completely dominating higher order retailing in the suburban ring and challenging the downtown area. The centres are augmented by a gridiron of urban arterial ribbons which serve not only the surrounding area but the larger region containing all the people who regularly drive that route, and a number of specialized commercial districts which are used by various sectors of the population throughout the metropolitan area.

Tables 7, 8, and 9 summarize the concentration of the different business types in the various parts of the commercial structure. Table 8 indicates

TABLE 7

BUSINESS TYPES BY AGGREGATION

Business Types	Total No. of Establishments	Centres						Ribbon and Scattered						Grand Total	
		Unplanned		Planned		Total		Unplanned		Planned		Total			
		G	U	G	U	G	U	G	U	G	U	G	U	G	U
Food	2474	488	....	87	....	575	....	1738	....	161	....	1899	....	2474	....
General	1021	183	6	46	....	229	6	732	....	54	....	786	....	1015	6
Auto	1891	150	....	18	....	168	....	1685	....	38	....	1723	....	1891	....
Clothes	1966	753	7	250	....	1003	7	769	13	173	1	942	14	1945	21
Furnishings	1419	342	1	76	....	418	1	915	5	79	1	994	6	1412	7
Other	2288	595	8	184	2	779	10	1326	17	153	3	1479	20	2258	30
Finance	1628	286	245	63	42	349	287	606	247	83	56	689	303	1038	590
Comm. Serv.	2763	200	357	45	62	245	419	952	936	79	132	1031	1068	1276	1487
Bus. Serv.	878	65	247	3	28	68	275	187	307	2	39	189	346	257	621
Pers. Serv.	5693	975	72	131	7	1106	79	4001	137	360	10	4361	147	5467	226
Miscellaneous	524	54	50	3	7	57	57	314	85	5	6	319	91	376	148
Total	22545	4091	993	906	148	4997	1141	13225	1747	1187	248	14412	1995	19409	3136
Vacancies	1540	171	98	30	15	201	113	922	191	68	45	990	236	1191	349
Deterioration	355	40	....	....	....	40	....	315	....	....	....	315	....	355	....

TABLE 8

BUSINESS TYPES BY AGGREGATION (PER CENT OF ALL BUSINESS TYPES)

Business Types	Establishments	Centres						Ribbon and Scattered						Grand Total	
		Unplanned		Planned		Total		Unplanned		Planned		Total			
		G	U	G	U	G	U	G	U	G	U	G	U	G	U
Food	2474	19.7	....	3.5	....	23.2	....	70.2	....	6.5	....	76.7	....	100.0	....
General	1021	17.9	0.6	4.5	....	22.4	0.6	71.8	....	5.3	....	77.1	....	99.5	0.6
Auto	1891	7.9	....	1.0	....	8.9	....	89.1	....	2.0	....	91.1	....	100.0	....
Clothes	1966	38.4	0.4	12.7	....	51.1	0.4	39.1	0.7	8.8	0.0	47.9	0.7	99.0	1.1
Furnishings	1419	24.1	0.1	5.4	....	29.5	0.1	64.6	0.4	5.6	0.1	70.2	0.5	99.7	0.6
Other	2288	26.1	0.4	8.1	0.1	34.2	0.5	58.2	0.8	6.7	0.1	64.9	0.9	99.1	1.4
Finance	1628	17.5	15.0	3.9	2.6	21.4	17.6	37.2	15.0	5.1	3.4	42.3	18.4	63.7	36.0
Community Service	2763	7.2	12.9	1.6	2.2	8.8	15.1	34.4	33.9	2.9	4.8	37.3	38.7	46.1	53.8
Business Serv.	878	7.4	28.1	0.3	3.2	7.7	31.3	21.3	35.0	0.2	4.4	21.5	39.4	29.2	70.7
Personal Service	5693	17.2	1.2	2.3	0.1	19.5	1.3	70.3	2.4	6.3	0.2	76.6	2.6	96.1	3.9
Miscellaneous	524	10.3	9.5	0.6	1.3	10.9	10.8	60.0	16.2	1.0	1.1	61.0	17.3	71.9	28.1
Total	22545	18.0	4.4	4.1	0.7	22.1	5.1	58.5	7.8	5.3	1.1	63.8	8.9	85.9	14.0
Vacancies	1540	11.1	6.4	1.9	1.0	13.0	7.3	59.9	12.4	4.4	2.9	64.2	15.3	77.3	22.6
Deteriorated	355	11.2	....	....	....	11.2	....	88.8	....	....	....	....	....	100.0	....

TABLE 9

BUSINESS TYPES BY AGGREGATION (PER CENT OF ALL AGGREGATIONS)

Business Types	Centres					
	Unplanned		Planned		Total	
	G	U	G	U	G	U
Food	12.0	.....	9.5	.....	11.5	......
General	4.5	0.6	5.0	.....	4.6	......
Auto	3.7	.....	2.0	.....	3.4	......
Clothes	18.4	0.7	27.3	.....	20.1	0.6
Furnishings	8.4	0.1	8.3	.....	8.4	0.1
Other	14.5	0.8	20.1	1.4	15.4	0.9
Finance	7.0	25.1	6.9	28.6	7.0	25.5
Community Service	4.9	37.5	4.9	42.2	4.9	37.3
Business Service	1.6	25.3	0.3	19.0	1.4	24.5
Personal Service	23.9	7.4	14.3	4.8	22.2	7.0
Miscellaneous	1.3	5.1	0.3	4.8	1.1	5.1
Total	4082	978	915	147	4997	1125
Vacancies	4.0	9.1	3.2	9.3	3.9	9.1
Deteriorations	1.0	.....	0.0	.....	......	......

TABLE 9--Continued

Ribbon and Scattered						Grand Total		
Unplanned		Planned		Total				
G	U	G	U	G	U	G	U	Total
13.2	......	13.4	.....	13.2	......	12.7	......	11.0
5.5	......	4.5	.....	5.5	......	5.2	0.2	4.5
12.7	......	3.5	.....	11.9	......	9.7	......	8.4
5.8	0.7	14.3	0.4	6.5	0.7	10.0	0.7	8.7
6.9	0.3	6.6	0.4	6.9	0.3	7.8	0.2	6.3
10.0	1.0	12.7	1.2	10.3	1.0	11.6	1.0	10.1
4.6	14.1	6.9	22.2	4.8	15.1	5.3	18.9	7.2
7.3	53.6	6.6	52.4	7.1	53.6	6.6	47.8	12.3
1.4	17.5	0.2	15.4	1.3	17.3	1.3	19.9	3.7
30.2	7.8	29.8	4.0	30.2	7.4	28.1	7.2	25.2
2.4	4.9	0.4	2.4	2.2	4.6	1.9	4.8	2.3
13217	1739	1204	252	14421	1991	19418	3116	22534
6.5	9.9	5.4	15.4	6.5	10.6	5.8	10.0	6.4
2.4	......	0.0	.....	....	......	1.8	......	....

the importance of the various forms of aggregation for the different business types. It should be noted that ribbon retailing is universally important, even for the higher order business types such as clothing. Planned centres are still only a small part of the total structure. Upper floor retailing is essential for certain services, business services in the centres and community services in the ribbons. Table 9 examines the importance of the various business types to the aggregations, i.e., the variations in the mix of commercial activities. Certain portions of the structure are quite vulnerable. Upper floor uses differ from ground floor and depend strongly on community services. A reduction in number or a changing location preference of this business type could create a serious blight problem. Ground floor ribbons lean on the personal service group, particularly restaurants. The planned centres are stronger in high order shopping goods, clothing, and other retail than their unplanned counterparts, as are the planned ribbons. A district dominated by planned centres will have proportionately more ribbon stores to provide low order activities.

Table 9 also reveals the pattern of the two blight characteristics, vacancies and deteriorations. Vacancies are a greater problem in upper floors, averaging almost 10 per cent even in planned centres. Unplanned centres have a lower vacancy rate than ribbons, although higher than planned centres. Deterioration, non-existent in planned centres, is more than twice as prevalent in unplanned ribbons than in unplanned centres.

Areal Aggregations

Census Tracts

The groupings of business types classified above are functional entities and their boundaries do not necessarily correspond to any of the spatial units into which the city has been divided for other data-gathering purposes. Because the information obtained from sources other than the field study was broken down by areas, the field data too was cross-classified into areal units. Since considerable use is made of census tract information, the field sheets were summarized on that basis, enabling retail characteristics to be compared to population characteristics and residential blight data. It is especially useful for those ribbon and scattered establishments which do not belong to any aggregation.

Zones of Analysis

Although information is available on the commercial activity and the
population characteristics of each census tract, the relationships between the
two sets of variables lose meaning because the tracts are too small. Residents
of the tract shop outside it; stores within the tract serve customers beyond
its borders. To overcome this problem the census tracts were aggregated into
fourteen zones, containing from 4 to 43 census tracts and from 30,000 to
240,000 people (1961). The zones were based to some extent on the Metro
Planning Board's planning districts but were modified in order to obtain census
tract boundaries which were unchanged between 1951 and 1961.

These zones will be important units in the analysis to follow in
Chapter III, but they are excellent descriptive units as well. Tables 10, 11,
and 12 show how the commercial structure varies across the study area. To aid
further in the interpretation, the zones themselves have been grouped into four
concentric rings according to their period of development: pre-war, post-war,
present, and future. (Maps and detailed summaries by zones are found in
Appendix C.) The first table shows how the types of aggregations vary among
zones. Particularly interesting is the pattern of variation in the growth
rings. Note the regular decline in importance of the unplanned centre and the
increasing role of the planned centre as one goes outward from the city centre
(except for the future ring where the definition of the outlying centres exag-
gerates their importance). The proportion of stores in centres decreases from
30 to 18 per cent, but the ground floor establishments remain relatively constant between 80 and 90 per cent. Table 11 examines the ground floor, upper
floor relationship more closely, indicating that the pattern is complex with
no discernible trends.

TABLE 10

COMMERCIAL AGGREGATIONS BY ZONES[1]

Zone	Name	Centres[2]					
		Unplanned		Planned		Total	
		G	U	G	U	G	U
I.	Central	214	29	.....	.....	214	29
II.	West End	878	106	45	3	923	109
III.	East End	662	66	54	.....	711	66
IV.	Uptown	1015	530	38	9	1053	539
V.	Lakeshore	136	29	.....	.....	136	29
VI.	Northwest	391	98	.....	.....	391	98
VII.	Scarboro S.	......	.....	113	19	113	19
VIII.	Etobicoke	126	24	123	19	259	43
IX.	N. York	97	27	157	18	254	45
X.	Bayview	4	.....	134	8	138	8
XI.	Scarboro N.	......	.....	80	29	80	29
XII.	Far West[2]	244	44	74	27	318	71
XIII.	Far North[2]	314	25	39	.....	353	25
XIV.	Far East[2]	......	.....	58	15	58	15
TOTAL		4081	978	915	147	5001	1125
Pre-war	(I, II, III, IV)	22.3	5.9	1.1	0.1	23.4	6.0
Post-war	(V, VI, VII)	14.0	3.4	3.0	0.5	17.0	3.9
Present	(VIII, IX, X, XI)	4.9	1.1	10.7	1.6	15.6	2.7
Future	(XII, XIII, XIV)	31.3	3.9	9.7	2.4	42.0	6.3
TOTAL		18.0	4.4	4.1	0.7	22.1	5.1

[1]More Complete zone data is found in Appendix C.

[2]Unplanned centres are the outlying centres.

TABLE 10--Continued

| Ribbon, Scattered, and Small Nucleations | | | | | | Grand Total | | |
| Unplanned | | Planned | | Total | | | | |
G	U	G	U	G	U	G	U	Total
1777	568	......	.....	1777	568	1991	597	2588
2419	121	......	.....	2419	121	3342	230	3572
2168	151	......	.....	2168	151	2884	217	3101
1307	259	20	2	1327	261	2378	800	3178
507	51	17	2	524	53	651	82	733
1336	73	23	4	1359	77	1738	175	1913
701	56	181	32	782	88	995	107	1102
640	87	230	52	870	139	1145	182	1327
1017	236	186	40	1203	276	1456	321	1787
291	54	205	29	496	83	634	91	725
303	54	220	71	523	125	634	154	788
440	25	63	17	503	42	821	113	934
196	4	45	3	241	7	594	32	626
115	......	14	.....	129	......	187	15	202
13217	1739	1204	252	14321	1991	19450	3166	22576
61.8	8.8	0.2	0.0	62.0	8.8	85.4	14.8	100.2
68.9	4.8	5.9	1.0	73.9	5.8	90.9	9.7	100.6
48.7	9.3	18.2	4.2	66.9	13.5	82.5	16.2	98.7
42.7	1.6	6.9	1.1	49.6	2.7	91.6	9.0	100.6
58.5	7.8	5.3	1.1	63.8	8.9	85.9	14.0	99.9

TABLE 11

UPPER FLOOR RETAILING (PER CENT OF TOTAL ESTABLISHMENTS)

| | Centres | | | Ribbons | | | |
	Unplanned	Planned	Total	Unplanned	Planned	Total	Total
Pre-war	20.9	2.1	20.4	12.5	9.1	12.5	17.4
Post-war	19.5	14.4	18.6	6.6	14.7	7.8	9.9
Present	18.3	6.2	14.6	16.1	18.6	16.8	16.4
Future	11.0	19.7	13.2	3.7	14.1	5.3	9.1
Total	19.5	14.0	18.6	11.7	17.3	12.2	13.9

The pattern of variation of business types is surprisingly consistent, considering that the facilities in each growth zone were constructed in equilibrium with a different set of socio-economic forces. Toward the outskirts, there is a decline in the proportion of food stores, a business type which has been reduced in number over time, and in clothing stores, which are high order stores with a preference for centrality. The proportion of financial institutions increases. Deterioration rates are lower for the newer areas, but high again in the future ring with its older outlying centres. At this gross level of measurement vacancy rates do not vary much across the study area.

TABLE 12

BUSINESS TYPES BY ZONES (1964)

Zone	Name	Total Estab.	Food	Auto	General	Clothes	Household
I.	Central	2588	271	87	135	189	157
II.	West End	3572	553	195	203	404	266
III.	East End	3101	389	187	247	279	231
IV.	Uptown	3178	269	84	172	258	180
V.	Lakeshore	733	69	47	56	58	56
VI.	Northwest	1913	235	111	173	195	127
VII.	Scarboro S.	1102	101	51	171	69	67
VIII.	Etobicoke	1327	111	46	140	117	78
IX.	N. York	1787	199	82	166	130	108
X.	Bayview	725	58	23	55	800	45
XI.	Scarboro N.	788	69	39	90	70	42
XII.	Far West	934	74	34	140	68	58
XIII.	Far North	626	53	20	112	40	56
XIV.	Far East	202	21	8	31	11	23
TOTAL		22576	2472	1014	1891	1968	1494
Pre-war	(I, II, III, IV)	12439	11.9%	4.4%	6.1%	9.1%	6.7%
Post-war	(V, VI, VII)	3748	10.8%	5.6%	10.7%	8.6%	6.7%
Present	(VIII, IX, X, XI)	4627	9.4%	4.1%	9.7%	8.6%	6.1%
Future	(XII, XIII, XIV)	1762	8.4%	3.5%	16.0%	6.8%	7.8%
TOTAL		22576	11.0%	4.5%	8.4%	8.7%	6.6%

TABLE 12--Continued

Other	Finance	Comm. Services	Business Services	Pers. Services	Misc.	Vacancy	Deteriorated
215	88	588	90	670	101	208	156
381	160	344	67	927	66	306	80
334	147	304	64	859	65	208	57
331	398	373	308	691	121	183	9
56	52	76	24	232	15	44	0
208	113	193	47	491	39	124	29
108	68	118	15	313	16	76	4
145	115	165	51	330	27	69	0
153	162	230	84	436	27	127	8
96	80	92	30	154	6	57	1
69	71	109	31	190	12	42	0
92	91	96	38	223	16	69	1
60	63	56	10	140	10	26	10
18	16	20	4	47	3	14	0
2266	1624	2764	871	5703	524	1545	355
10.1%	6.4%	12.9%	4.2%	25.3%	2.8%	6.78%	2.42%
9.9%	7.2%	10.3%	2.3%	27.6%	1.9%	6.11%	0.87%
10.0%	9.2%	12.9%	4.2%	24.0%	1.6%	5.83%	0.19%
9.6%	9.5%	9.8%	3.4%	23.2%	1.6%	5.82%	0.62%
10.1%	7.2%	12.3%	3.9%	25.2%	2.3%	6.40%	1.57%

CHAPTER III

BLIGHT

The complex commercial structure detailed in the last chapter has
evolved through time to meet the needs of the metropolitan population. A major
hypothesis of this study is that there is a strong interrelation between the
retail and service facilities and the consumers. As a result, a period of
rapid change in the urban population creates stress and imbalance in the commercial structure, leading to blight.

The Distribution and Characteristics of Consumers

Chapter I gave some hint of the rapid growth in numbers (from 1,100,000
to 1,600,000 in Metro in the period 1951-1961, an annual increase of 3.8 per
cent), but there has been great qualitative change as well. The earnings of a
wage-earner family head have increased from $2653 (median) to $4746 (average);[1]
the number of automobiles per 1000 from 22.1 per cent to 31.6 per cent; and the
proportion of non-British origin from 27.3 per cent to 40.7 per cent of the
Metro Toronto population. These net changes for the area as a whole mask much
more complex alterations in the spatial patterns of these characteristics
throughout the metropolitan area. For instance, Figure 9, which shows population change by census tract, indicates considerable areas of declining population despite the overall pattern of growth.

The Special Census Analysis

A valuable tool in describing consumer distribution is the technique of
factor analysis. During the same period as the commercial study the
Metropolitan Toronto Urban Renewal Study commissioned a special census analysis
in which the available census data for the metropolitan area were factor
analyzed to provide information about the socio-economic characteristics of

---

[1]Unfortunately, the only detailed source of information about income,
the census, changed from a median to an average measurement during the decade.
When the median is obtained by interpolation from tables of income groups
(Census of Canada, 1961, Table 4-1-6, F-1 and F-8) it runs about 75 per cent of
the average. Using this ratio the median income has increased from $2650 to
$3550, an annual change of 3.0 per cent. If the cost of living increase of 1.3
per cent is deducted, the annual change in real income is approximately 1.7 per
cent. This income includes only wage and salary income which is augmented by
welfare payments in the poorer areas and investment income in the wealthier
districts.

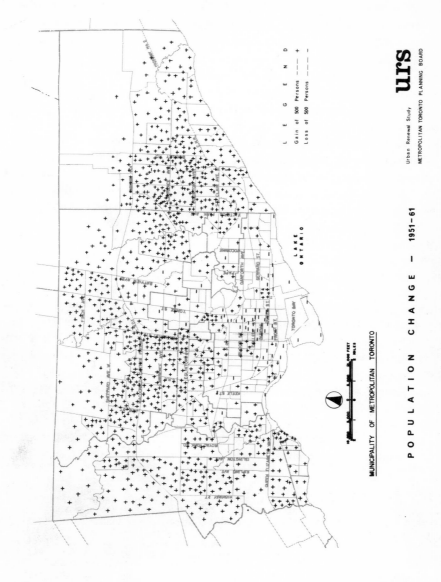

MUNICIPALITY OF METROPOLITAN TORONTO

POPULATION CHANGE – 1951–61

L E G E N D

Gain of 500 Persons ———— +

Loss of 500 Persons ———— –

urs

Urban Renewal Study

METROPOLITAN TORONTO PLANNING BOARD

Fig. 9.—Population Change—1951–61

blight. The results, which summarize the information of 75 different variables within six or seven factors, describe the Metropolitan population very efficiently.[1]

The forms of blight identified in Chapter I result in varying degrees from the interaction of the two distributions, commercial facilities, and consumer characteristics.

Physical Blight

Deteriorated Buildings

The most direct measure of physical blight is the distribution of deteriorated commercial buildings. This definition conforms to that used in the other surveys by the Metropolitan Toronto Urban Renewal Study Group, based on the standard Dominion Bureau of Statistics definition used in the census. Only structural deterioration is considered, defined as faults which would require major alteration to correct, such as sagging roofs, walls out of plumb, crumbling brick work, rotten foundations, etc. Figures 10 and 11 show the distribution of deteriorated commercial establishments and the percentage of deterioration by census tract. Physical blight is highly concentrated (see histogram) in the old core of the city and along the older arterial roads leading out of the city (Highway No. 2 East and West and Weston Road) where there has been a long history of commercial development in small crossroads centres. A comparison with Figure 3 shows the importance of these early centres as sources of deteriorated buildings. The major exception to this pattern is Yonge Street where continued renewal by the private sector in a high income area has eliminated most of the evidence of the deterioration which might be expected.

Table 9 revealed that throughout the study area the unplanned centres averaged 1.0 per cent deterioration compared to the 2.4 per cent rate for unplanned ribbons, while planned centres are still too new to be subject to

---

[1]Since the factor analysis results are used in the analysis to follow they are found in Appendix D. For more detailed discussions consult Brian J. L. Berry and Robert Murdie, Report on the Special Census Analysis for the Metropolitan Toronto Urban Renewal Study, Toronto, 1965. The most complete discussion will be the book by Robert Murdiewhich will appear in the University of Chicago Research Series. Factor analysis has been used to explain retail patterns in Berry and Tennant, Metropolitan Planning Guidelines: Commercial Structure, Appendix A, where its use in urban socio-economic analysis is reviewed in some detail. See also T. R. Anderson and J. E. Egeland, "Spatial Aspects of Social Area Analysis," American Sociological Review, XXVI (1961) pp. 392-398; and Brian J. L. Berry, "Cities as Systems within Systems of Cities", Papers and Proceedings of the Regional Science Association, XI (1963), forthcoming.

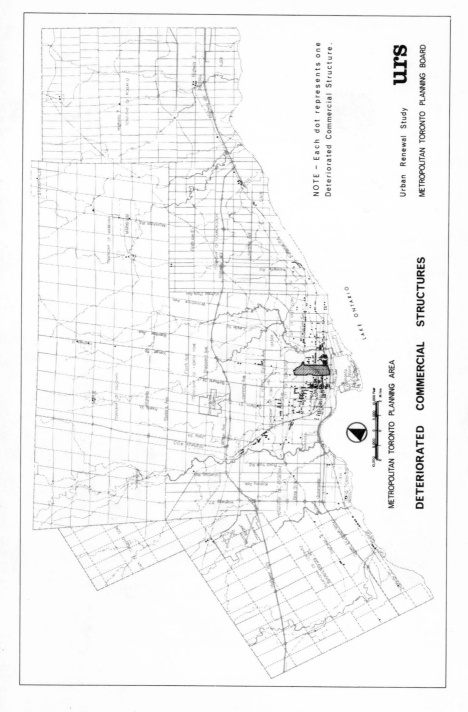

Fig. 10.--Deteriorated Commercial Structures

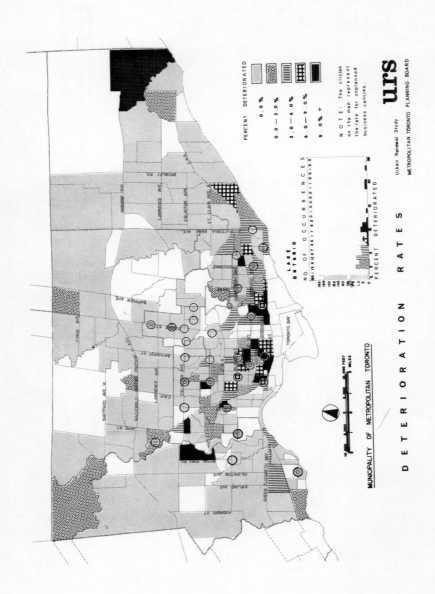

Fig. 11.—Deterioration Rates

these structural defects. Although the deterioration rates appear low, twenty-two census tracts and two centres (Queen-Bathurst, Queen-Landsdowne) have more than 8 per cent of their buildings in this condition. Generally speaking, the deterioration of individual centres does not differ greatly from the immediately surrounding ribbon except for three centres (Weston, Yonge-Castleford, Queen-Lee) which were early commercial areas.

Relationship to
Other Forms of Blight

Physical blight is due primarily to the age of the structure, but it may also result from poor original construction, such as is found in lower income areas, or poor maintenance. This last factor relates physical blight to economic, functional, and frictional blight, all of which reduce the store income and forestall investment in repairs, and may also be expected to result in commercial vacancies. However the map of vacant stores (Figures 12 and 13) indicates that the gross patterns of occurrence of vacancies and deteriorated buildings are quite independent.[1] Vacancies are much more widely dispersed, reaching all portions of the planning area, with 50 tracts greater than 9 per cent vacant (compared to the study area vacancy rate of 6.5 per cent). Although there is an overall concentration of both vacancy and deterioration rates in Zones I, II, and III, the correlation between the two variables for census tracts in Zone I is only 0.37, not significant at the 0.95 (one-tail) level. Table 2 also indicates that high deteriorations do not necessarily lead to high vacancy rates or vice versa. However, a relationship exists at the level of the individual establishment where 25 per cent of the total of 365 deteriorated buildings are vacant, suggesting that the economic selection process tends to eliminate physically inadequate facilities from the market for retail space. Where better structures are available businesses will move to them, abandoning the deteriorated buildings.

Economic Blight

Commercial vacancies indicate a surplus of commercial space, an imbalance in the supply and demand for retail and service facilities. A certain amount of vacancies, perhaps 3 or 4 per cent, result from the turnover of

---

[1]The definition of vacancy is complicated by the existence of new construction, i.e., buildings vacant because they are still being completed. The line is drawn between those new buildings which are ready and those which are not ready for occupancy. In some cases such as Yorkdale, however, stores with incomplete interiors are listed as vacant, since the centre is almost complete and is functioning.

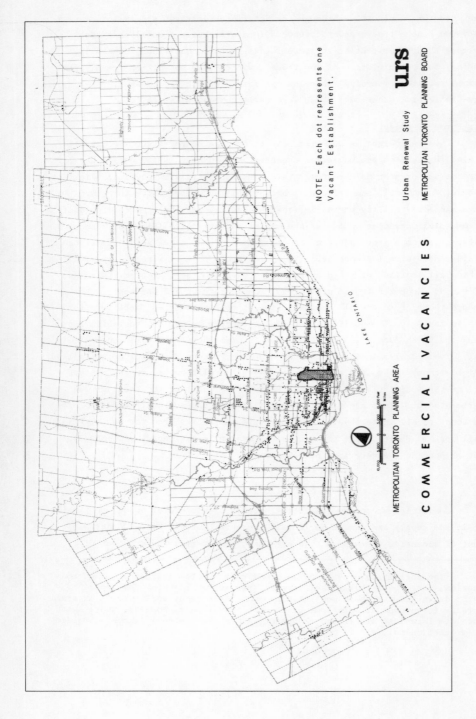

Fig. 12.--Commercial Vacancies

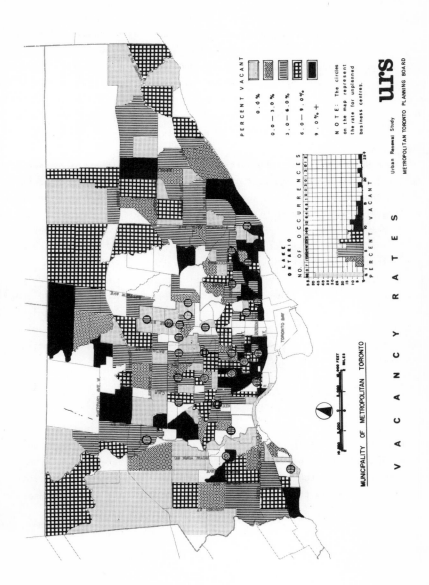

Fig. 13.--Vacancy Rate

commercial facilities, but beyond that the vacancies resulting from insufficient demand may be termed economic blight. Vacant stores are widely spread across the study area.

The Outer Fringe

Towards the outskirts of the city the sparseness of commercial development, together with a trend to planned centres which are built as units, creates unevenness in the distribution of commercial establishments. There are also temporary imbalances between commercial and residential construction. The result is a wide disparity in vacancy rates--from 0.0 per cent to over 12 per cent--which will disappear given sufficient time for adjustment, since Table 12 shows that the overall vacancy rate is low in this part of the study area.

The Inner City

Much more serious are the cores of high vacancies in the older sections of the city: an area east and west of the central business district; another out Weston Road south of Weston; and small problem areas in Etobicoke on Bloor and at Long Branch. Throughout these older areas there is a great diversity in vacancy rates within zones and among clusters of stores in adjacent tracts which may reflect local variations in population growth, the introduction of new competitors, or perhaps the functional specialization of the various commercial aggregations, since some types of business have been more seriously affected by technological change than others. A sharp contrast to these areas is the zone of very low vacancy rates on Yonge north where population and incomes have been steadily rising. Vacancy rates in unplanned centres are consistently lower than the surrounding ribbons although there is no indication that the centres have any detrimental effect on the latter.

The Relationship Between Retail Facilities and Consumer Characteristics

To evaluate the demand and supply imbalance, the relationship between consumer requirements and retail facilities must be precisely defined. Using the zones of analysis as measurement units, a series of regression equations was developed treating the various retail characteristics as dependent variables to be predicted by the population characteristics. The variables used and the regression equations are listed in Appendix E, but the highlights of these relationships are listed here.[1]

Explanation by
the Factor Scores

The measure of retail activity is the number of establishments in the various functional categories as ascertained in the field study (field survey sheet, Appendix A) for each zone. These measures were related to the population, income level, and the average score of the zone first on the three leading factors and then on the seven leading factors derived from the 1961 census analysis (Appendix D). Thus there are four sets of equations of increasing complexity which give increasing amounts of information:

(1)   Retail Variable = f(population)

(2)   = f(population, income)

(3)   = f(population, I, II, III)

(4)   = f(population, I, II, III, IV, V, VI, VII)

Eighty-three per cent of the total variation in the total number of establishments is explained by population as shown in Table 13. However, this variable alone is not sufficient to explain the spatial distribution of particular types of commercial activity. Finance, community and business services, and miscellaneous establishments are only slightly responsive to population variation. These specialized uses cluster together to serve certain sectors of the population over a large part of the metropolitan area. For these uses, the factor scores of consumer characteristics greatly increase prediction. Part of this increase is the effect of a large number of explanatory variables in a system with a small number of observations, but sufficient meaningful relationships exist to prove the worth of these independent variables. Table 14 indicates that all factors contribute to the explanation, although factors I through III do the bulk of the work. The aggregation into observation units larger than those used in the factor analysis introduces a certain amount of intercorrelation between the factor scores, but not above the 0.5 level.

---

[1]The factors are identified as:
      I   Low socio-economic level
     II Suburban family   } (3)
   III Good household amenities
    IV Anglo-Saxon Protestant   (4)
     V Residential stability
    VI Central European
  VII Boarding house

TABLE 13

EXPLANATION BY DIFFERENT VARIABLES (r^2)

Dependent Variable	(1) f(Population)	(2) f(Population, Income)	(3) f(Population, Three Factor Scores)	(4) f(Population, Seven Factor Scores)
All establishments	0.832	0.864	0.988	0.992
Food	.808	.916	.947	.977
Auto	.827	.946	.961	.978
General	.743	.758	.772	.833
Clothing	.841	.877	.927	.975
Household	.828	.908	.966	.981
Other	.872	.884	.970	.990
Finance	.445	.572	.828	.929
Community Service	.389	.458	.878	.934
Business Service	.262	.352	.785	.904
Personal Service	.830	.897	.987	.993
Miscellaneous	0.426	0.442	0.933	0.945

TABLE 14

PARTIAL CORRELATION COEFFICIENTS

Dependent Variable	Population	(Low Socio-economic Level) I	(Suburban Family) II	(Good Household Amenities) III	(Anglo-Saxon Protestant) IV	(Residential Stability) V	(Central European) VI	(Boarding House) VII
Total Estab.	0.931	- 0.611	- 0.914	- 0.900	- 0.197	0.130	0.484	- 0.029
Food	.799	.627	- .345	- .657	.437	.352	.661	.342
Auto	.729	.881	- .315	.026	- .332	.553	.186	.546
General	.431	.338	.300	.131	- .265	.373	- .404	.219
Clothing	.657	.158	- .621	- .338	- .616	.595	.668	.533
Household	.820	.281	- .718	- .715	- .298	.497	.437	.342
Other	.857	- .552	- .851	- .614	- .643	.741	.280	.567
Finance	.775	- .909	- .775	- .568	.479	- .507	- .051	- .702
Community Services	.520	- .279	- .730	- .816	- .042	- .368	- .051	- .018
Business Services	.714	- .902	- .824	- .716	.571	- .598	- .039	- .716
Personal Services	.924	.419	- .910	- .881	.107	.436	.558	.301
Miscellaneous	0.628	- 0.790	- 0.885	- 0.835	- 0.325	- 0.274	- 0.010	- 0.390

Effect of Specific Factors.--There are two alternative explanations for these relationships. First, direct causal links exist between certain types of stores and certain population characteristics which affect demand. It can be shown that the mix of goods purchased by a family varies with family size, family income, and family age.[1] On the other hand, spatial relationships emerge because of similar location requirements, although there may be no direct consumer-store relationships. For instance, the data indicate that there may be direct links between the location of the business and the residence of the owner or manager rather than the customers. Other evidence leading to this hypothesis emerges from Zimmer's work on store relocation which indicates that, first, the process of business location is not particularly rational in the sense of optimizing access to customers; second, the social characteristics of entrepreneurs vary consistently by business type; and third, there is a tendency for store relocations to take place towards the owner's residence.[2]

Detailed examination of the effect of the various factors shows that food, automobile, and personal service activities are proportionately greater in low income areas; shopping goods and financial, business, and commercial services are especially concentrated in wealthier districts. Nearly all kinds of stores are negatively related to the family structure factor which is, in turn, negatively related to the population of zones. The latter relation results from the smaller population of the suburban zones as they have been defined for this study. The former correlation indicates that the retail structure is more highly concentrated than the distribution of consumers. The suburbs have a less than proportionate share of the total number of stores. The same sort of coincidence creates the high negative relation of stores and factor three. The area of poor housing in the older part of the city is an area of commercial concentration, particularly specialized functional areas--professional, business services, Kensington Market, and furniture. Column four indicates that concentrations of financial and business service activities are found in the Anglo-Saxon Protestant areas, and clothing and other retailing in the Jewish-Polish districts which are at the other end of the scale. Factor five, residential stability, has the same pattern as automobile, clothing,

---

[1]Simmons, The Changing Pattern of Retail Locations, Chapter V.

[2]Basil G. Zimmer, Rebuilding Cities, The Effects of Displacement and Relocation on Small Business (Chicago: Quadrangle Books, 1964), Chapters III, IV, and V.

furniture, and other retailing groups and is negatively linked to financial, community, and business services. Concentration of Central European populations (VI) correlates with food, clothing, and personal service groups; and factor seven is associated with the automobile, clothing, and other retail groups.

The Business Centres

Similarly, regression relationships may be established for the centres, and since they are meaningful integrated commercial aggregations, relationships between retail characteristics of centres may be examined as well. The equations below relate business types and establishments in centres:[1]

Unplanned Centres

(4.1) Ground Floor

$$\text{Log Est.} = 1.51 + 0.0115 \text{ BT} \qquad (r^2 = 0.71)$$
$$(0.0014)$$

(4.2) Upper Floor

$$\text{Log Est.} = 0.698 + 0.0537 \text{ BT} \qquad (r^2 = 0.80)$$
$$(0.0051)$$

Planned Centres

(4.3) Ground Floor

$$\text{Log Est} = 1.10 + 0.0165 \text{ BT} \qquad (r^2 = 0.90)$$
$$(0.0013)$$

(4.4) Upper Floor

$$\text{Log Est} = 0.165 + 0.1095 \text{ BT} \qquad (r^2 = 0.82)$$
$$(0.0123)$$

These equations reveal that there is considerable regularity in centre characteristics: unplanned centres have more establishments than planned centres; and the number of upper floor establishments in either centre type rises more rapidly as the number of business types increase than do the ground floor establishments. In addition, the correlation matrices (Table 15) indicate that for both kinds of centres vacancy rates are independent of scale; and the degree

---

[1]These results may be compared with the relationships derived for the Chicago centres (Simmons, p. 162 ff.):
Unplanned Centres
$$\text{Log Est} = 1.19 + 0.0188 \text{ BT} \qquad (r^2 = 0.83)$$
Planned Centres
$$\text{Log Est} = 0.80 + 0.0276 \text{ BT} \qquad (r^2 = 0.91)$$
and the Chicago suburban centres (Berry and Tennant, Appendix B):
Unplanned Centres
$$\text{Log Est} = 1.15 + 0.0161 \text{ BT} \qquad (r^2 = 0.96)$$
Despite the variations in local conditions the relationships are quite consistent.

TABLE 15

CORRELATION MATRICES FOR CENTRES

	Ground Floor			Upper Floor	
	Business Types	Log. Establishments	Vacancy Rate	Business Types	Log. Establishments
Unplanned Centres (N = 29)					
Ground Floor — Business Types	1.000				
Ground Floor — Log. Establishments	.841	1.000			
Ground Floor — Vacancy Rate	-.265	-.338	1.000		
Upper Floor — Business Types	-.018	-.010	-.039	1.000	
Upper Floor — Log. Establishments	.012	-.004	-.098	.896	1.000
Planned Centres (N - 20)					
Ground Floor — Business Types	1.000				
Ground Floor — Log. Establishments	.946	1.000			
Ground Floor — Vacancy Rate	.258	.248	1.000		
Upper Floor — Business Types	-.449	-.365	-.162	1.000	
Upper Floor — Log Establishments	-.604	-.555	-.179	.903	1.000

degree of upper floor commercial use is completely unrelated to the amount of ground floor activity. Analysis of the distribution of upper floor uses must take into account completely different requirements and uses from the ground floor, higher order, stores.

Short-run Change

The concept of economic blight depends on the relationships detailed in the section above. Given a strong interdependence between commercial activity and consumer characteristics, a change in the latter must necessarily affect retail and service structure. The impact of the changes within Toronto is seen in Figure 14 which shows the net change in total number of retail and service establishments, 1951-1961.[1] Despite a general pattern of increase (4791 stores in Metro Toronto), there are pockets of decline, and these, as one might expect, are related to the pattern of vacancy rates in Figure 13.

The gross changes in the amount of stores and sales by zone may be related to shifts in population and income using the data of Table 26, Appendix C (summarized in Table 16). Note first that there is no zone of serious depopulation, at least at the scale of our units of observation. Zones I, II, and III are reasonably stable and the rest increase at from 1 per cent to 28 per cent per annum. Second, although the measures of income used indicate a mean annual per cent increase of 5.7 per cent for Metro, part of the increase is due to the shift from a median to an average measure and another part results from the increased cost of living. The increase in real income is about 1.7 per cent. There is relatively little variation among zones.

Two sets of equations are derived, relating changes in stores (ΔE), sales (ΔS), population (ΔP) and sales (ΔS). First, using absolute numbers:

$$(4.5) \quad \Delta E = 121.0 + 0.00410 \ \Delta P + 0.05201 \ \Delta I \quad (r^2 = 0.68)$$
$$ (0.00152) \quad\ \ (0.07928)$$

$$(4.6) \quad \Delta S(000'S) = 61800 + 0.5454 \ \Delta P - 2.5980 \ \Delta I \quad (r^2 = 0.41)$$
$$ (0.2875) \quad\ \ (15.032)$$

---

[1]Changes in the Dominion Bureau of Statistics' retail and service categories make it difficult to use any finer groupings.

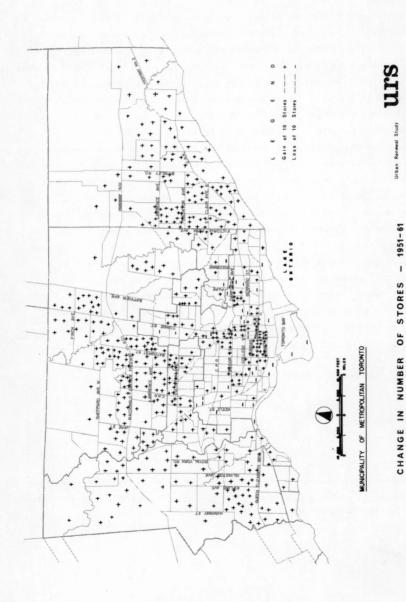

CHANGE IN NUMBER OF STORES – 1951–61

MUNICIPALITY OF METROPOLITAN TORONTO

Urban Renewal Study
METROPOLITAN TORONTO PLANNING BOARD

Fig. 14.—Changes in the Number of Stores--1951-1961

TABLE 16

MEAN ANNUAL PER CENT CHANGE BY ZONE
(1951-1961)

Zone	Population	Income[a]	Sales[b]			Stores			Ground Floor Vacancy Rate
			Observed	Predicted[c]	Residual	Observed	Predicted[d]	Residual	
I Central	-0.8	3.0	4.9	3.4	1.5	0.7	0.0	0.7	7.9
II West End	0.6	3.3	2.9	4.6	-1.7	0.5	1.4	-0.9	7.0
III East End	0.4	4.5	2.9	7.2	-4.3	0.7	1.2	-0.5	6.5
IV Uptown	1.1	5.3	5.6	9.3	-3.7	2.6	1.9	0.7	3.8
V Lakeshore	3.6	4.5	7.1	8.4	-1.3	2.1	4.2	-2.1	5.4
VI Northwest	2.1	3.3	3.0	5.2	-2.2	1.5	2.8	-1.3	5.5
VII Scarboro S.	10.8	6.0	19.2	14.5	4.7	13.7	11.0	2.7	5.5
VIII Etobicoke	12.4	5.2	18.6	13.3	5.3	14.5	12.4	2.1	3.5
IX N. York	12.1	5.2	19.7	13.2	6.5	14.1	12.2	1.9	6.0
X Bayview	14.9	7.0	21.5	18.3	3.2	12.7	14.8	-2.1	4.1
XI Scarboro N.	28.7	7.4	16.6	24.4	-7.8	26.5	27.7	-1.2	4.4
Total Metro Toronto	3.8	5.7	6.0	....	....	2.6	....	....	5.0

[a]Including the effect of shifting from a median to an average measure of income, and a 1.3 per cent per annum increase in the cost of living.

[b]Not corrected for the increased cost of living.

[c]Predicted by Equation 4.8.

[d]Predicted by Equation 4.7.

Converting these changes to annual per cent increase (the geometric mean) much more useful relationships are obtained.[1]

$$(4.7) \quad i_e = 0.673 + 0.934 \underset{(0.130)}{i_p} + 0.036 \underset{(0.802)}{i_i} \quad (r^2 = 0.96)$$

$$i_s = -3.04 + 0.376 \underset{(0.344)}{i_p} + 2.25 \underset{(2.13)}{i_i} \quad (r^2 = 0.67)$$

In either form, the prediction of sales is poorer than that of stores. Equation 4.7 may be interpreted as a tendency toward a slight increase in the number of stores in a given area, modified by an almost one-to-one relationship with population change, and unaffected by income change.

Sales, on the other hand, tend to decline unless bolstered by increase in population and income within the zone. The rate of decline in sales increases (from −3.0 per cent to −4.3 per cent) if the effect of inflation is considered. However, a zone which undergoes no population change and increases its income level by the metropolitan average rate of 5.7 per cent will show an annual increase in sales of 8.5 per cent.

Further insights are obtained by examination of the residuals from the regressions provided in Table 16. The definite pattern which emerges indicates that our equation is inadequate to provide full explanation of the change. For both stores and sales there is underprediction for the Central Zone, overprediction for Zones II to VI, and underprediction for the rest except Zone XI. The equilibrium pattern for the area as a whole has changed, and although Zone I continues to attract specialized commercial activities despite its stability of population, there has been a general transfer of retail activity from the older parts of the city to the newer suburbs at a rate more than proportional to their

---

[1]Again the regression equations may be compared to the Chicago results for similar units of analysis (Simmons, p. 69ff).

$$i_e = -5.87 + 0.978 \underset{(0.160)}{i_p} + 0.864 \underset{(0.298)}{i_i} \quad (r^2 = 0.93)$$

$$i_s = -4.63 + 1.513 \underset{(0.325)}{i_p} + 1.555 \underset{(0.599)}{i_i} \quad (r^2 = 0.90)$$

The Chicago analysis was restricted to the older parts of the city and included retail establishments only. The latter effect accounts for the difference in the value of the intercepts in the first equation. The effect of population change is the same, however, although the Toronto results showed income shifts to be much less important. In the sales equation, the intercepts are both strongly negative although the relative effects of population and income are different. In Toronto, stress is introduced by rapid growth; in Chicago, by the movement of low-income groups.

growth. Zone XI, the exception, still depends on nearby zones. Taking equations 4.7 and 4.8 together, there is a general pattern of declining sales which has been more than offset by the increasing incomes throughout the city. The increase in income has bolstered sales sufficiently to maintain the number of stores in areas of stable population despite the long-run trend to greater sales per store.

Since no zone has suffered a net decline in either stores or sales or has undergone serious depletion of population or income, it is difficult to attribute commercial vacancies to short-run changes in demand. It is possible that smaller observational units might show declines in potential sales which could lead to losses of stores and sales. Certainly such units would show higher vacancy rates. However, for the zones used in this analysis, the most important effect is the long-run shift in supply conditions which leads to outward movement of retail facilities. As disproportiona ely greater commercial growth takes place in the newer zones, less than proportionate increases take place in Zones I, II, and III, and areas which do not attract new investment are particularly vulnerable to obsolescence.

Functional Blight

The effect of the shifts in parameters mentioned above is really a type of functional blight, or obsolescence.[1] This form of blight includes a number of long-run trends operating throughout the study area at various levels of the commercial structure. Better highway access and increased automobile ownership, improving the mobility of the consumer, are shifting the balance among the major elements of the structure. The universal concern for the central business district is evidence of this trend. The increased mobility coupled with technological innovation introduces economies of scale, changing the relationships between sales, stores, and population. For instance, a new supermarket in an older area may replace half a dozen corner groceries. There are also fundamental changes in the nature of consumer demand, as indicated in the Special Census Analysis (Appendix D). The age structure is different, incomes higher, and ethnic origin more varied. Consumer preference changes over time: people buy different goods and require different merchandising techniques and services. The locations of many stores are obsolete, too. The accessibility of

---

[1]Hans Blumenfeld develops this theme of obsolescence in his paper "Obsolescence and Renewal in Canadian Cities," mimeo (Toronto, 1964).

store to pedestrian traffic becomes congestion in the eyes of the customer in
an automobile. Their clientele becomes more widely dispersed. New through
streets and expressways pass them by. Above all they lack the parking space
which new shopping plazas and ribbon stores supply so freely.

These various forms of obsolescence put older stores in a difficult
competitive position. In economic terms, the advantages of ready-made buildings and organizations are no longer sufficient to compete with economies of
scale and the attractions of access and parking. In an area of stable population and income the introduction of new stores, putting old ones out of
business, may create a high vacancy rate without changing the total number of
stores or sales. It is difficult to anticipate precisely the areas affected by
these forms of blight, but we can examine the degree to which these changes are
taking place throughout the metropolitan area.

The Changing Way of Life

Table 17 examines long-run trends in these influential variables.
Especially important are the increased mobility and the greater spending power
of the consumer whose real wages have increased by 40 per cent between 1951 and
1961. The best evidence of the change in mobility comes from another study in
Chicago which examined the shopping patterns of suburban housewives over time
and concluded, "The consumer is no longer locked into one or two locations but
by virtue of the automobile is free to visit a multiplicity of outlets."[1]
Stores are dealing with a much larger trade area and customers are dealing with
a whole range of centres. The income increase shifts the mix of goods which
the customer will buy toward transportation, recreation and clothing purchases.[2]
Retailing technology is also changing: the population served and the amount of
sales per store is increasing rapidly as customer mobility makes economies of
scale more attractive.

Figure 15 shows the changing demographic structure of Toronto between
1951 and 1961. Although the city's total population has not changed appre-
ciably it has increased the number of children and aged, while declining for
ages between 15 and 70. Old people increase medical services expenditures;

---

[1]Chicago Tribune, How Chicago Shops: The Changing Retail Market
(Chicago, 1964), p. 1. Their evidence indicates that the number of centres
regularly visited by a customer has risen sharply within the last ten years.

[2]The effects of age, income and family size are discussed more fully in
Simmons, The Changing Pattern of Retail Location, pp. 76, 77.

TABLE 17

THE CHANGING WAY OF LIFE

	Consumer's Weekly Price Index[a]	Wages and Salaries[b]	Wage Index[c]	Auto- mobiles per 1000 People[d]	Metropolitan Toronto[e]			
					Population	Stores	Sales (000's)	Sales/ Store[f]
1931	67.9	$			814,700	14,227	446,899 [f]	$46,300
1932	61.7						(658,000)	
1933	58.8							
1934	59.6							
1935	59.9							
1936	61.1							
1937	63.0							
1938	63.7			140				
1939	63.2	25.05	89.9	144				
1940	65.7	26.20	90.4	142				
1941	69.6	28.07	91.5	143	909,900	16,311	499,456	44,100
1942	72.9	29.75	92.7	139			(718,000)	
1943	74.2	31.79	97.4	135				
1944	74.6	32.69	99.4	132				
1945	75.0	32.66	99.0	128				
1946	77.5	33.12	97.1	136				
1947	84.8	37.02	99.0	147				
1948	97.0	41.00	96.1	160				
1949	100.0	44.04	100.0	188				
1950	102.9	46.49	102.3	206				
1951	113.7	51.68	103.4	221	1,117,500	15,932	1,405,497	78,500
1952	116.5	56.65	110.6	250			(1,236,000)	
1953	115.5	60.23	118.6	255				
1954	116.2	62.43	122.0	260				
1955	116.4	64.54	125.9	266				
1956	118.1	67.61	130.0	274	1,358,000			
1957	121.9	70.88	131.9	285				
1958	125.1	73.96	134.2	290				
1959	126.5	76.57	137.4	302				
1960	128.0	78.98	139.9	308				
1961	129.2	81.60	143.3	315	1,618,800	20,723	2,582,531	96,500
1962	130.7	84.10	146.2	318			(2,000,000)	

[a]Dominion Bureau of Statistics, Canadian Statistical Review, Historical Summary (1963), Table 31.

[b]Ibid. Table 25. Figures are for Toronto.

[c]Wages corrected for cost of living, relative to 1949 = 100.

[d]Draft Official Plan of the Metropolitan Toronto Planning Area (1959), plate 37, augmented by the Report on the Metropolitan Toronto Transportation Plan (1964), Figure 12.

[e]Dominion Bureau of Statistics, Census of Canada.

[f]Sales corrected to 1949 dollars.

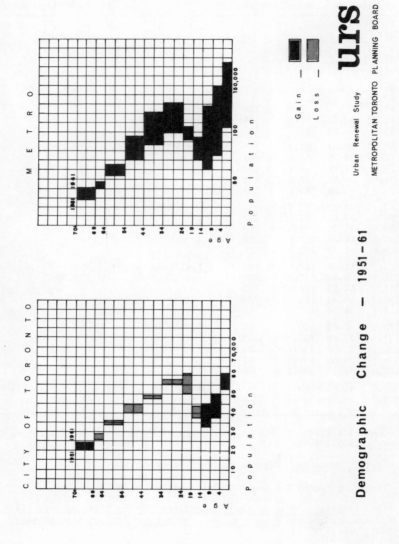

64

Demographic Change — 1951-61

Urban Renewal Study
METROPOLITAN TORONTO PLANNING BOARD

Fig. 15.--Demographic Change--1951-1961

large families spend disproportionate amounts on food and clothing. For Metro
as a whole there is an especially high growth rate in the age groups under 15
and 24-44, the young families who will spend money on food, clothes, and services rather than transportation, furniture, or housing.

Changing Parameters

The impact on the commercial structure of these changes in the way-of-
life of the average Torontonian is considerable. In an earlier section we
examined the consumer-retail facilities relationship in a dynamic sense, seek-
ing the effect of shifts of population and income on stores and sales, and
found that short-run changes were of less importance than the trend toward
suburbanization of commercial facilities. Long-run changes such as these may
also be examined by comparing the system as it appeared at two different points
in time. Using census data, the 1951 commercial structure may be related to
the consumer characteristics just as was done for the 1961 data:[1]

$$(4.8) \quad 1951 \quad E = 1341 + 0.01328\ P - 0.4966\ I \qquad (r^2 = 0.96)$$
$$(0.00110) \quad (0.1943)$$

$$(4.9) \quad S\ (000's) = 29270 + 0.8348\ P - 10.80\ I \quad (r^2 = 0.97)$$
$$(0.0582) \quad (10.30)$$

$$(4.10) \quad S\ (000's) = 9700 + 58.2\ E \qquad (r^2 = 0.95)$$

$$(4.11) \quad 1961 \quad E = 1190 + 0.01329\ P - 0.3080\ I \qquad (r^2 = 0.89)$$
$$(0.00154) \quad (0.0940)$$

$$(4.12) \quad S\ (000's) = 24150 + 1.059\ P - 4.033\ I \quad (r^2 = 0.82)$$
$$(0.149) \quad (9.069)$$

$$(4.13) \quad S\ (000's) = 39700 + 69.5\ E \qquad (r^2 = 0.84)$$

The income factor is negative in each case and of little significance in pre-
dicting sales. In the over-all commercial structure there is a high concentration of activity in older low-income areas near downtown which outweigh the
negative effect of lower purchasing power in these areas. This effect is more
significant for stores than for sales, since there are many small establishments

---

[1]The comparable equations for Chicago (Simmons, p. 72):

$$1948 \quad E = 1492 + 0.01043\ P - 13.31\ I\ (relative\ to\ 100) \quad (r^2 = 0.90)$$
$$(0.00186) \quad (26.44)$$

$$S\ (000's) = -143,300 + 0.849\ P + 1.187\ I \qquad (r^2 = 0.92)$$
$$(0.072) \quad (1.030)$$

$$1958 \quad E = 899 + 0.00733\ P - 4.414\ I \qquad (r^2 = 0.84)$$
$$(0.00157) \quad (16.46)$$

$$S\ (000's) = -258,300 + 1.078\ P + 2.540\ I \qquad (r^2 = 0.95)$$
$$(0.108) \quad (1.130)$$

Different parameters arise from the two studies because different measures were
used, but the trends are the same.

in these areas. The 1951 relationships are stronger in each case, perhaps indicating a more complex system in 1961 with greater metropolitan-wide purchasing.

Functional blight results from the changes in parameters in these equations over time. For instance, the relationship between stores and sales indicates that the sales/store are increasing, i.e., store size, putting pressure on stores in any area of stable consumer demand. On the other hand, the sales per person are increasing as the over-all income level goes up. The other equation, relating stores to income and population, seems quite stable with a slight decline in the intercept. The decline in the size of the income parameter is compensated by the increase as mean income is substituted for median income in 1961.

The residuals from these regressions (Table 18) indicate that the model is a bit rough for predictive purposes, or in other words, the system is too complex for the model. There is consistent underprediction in the central zone where there is a concentration of stores dealing with a metropolitan-wide trade area, and overprediction for many of the other zones, except for those with high incomes--Etobicoke, Bayview, and the Far West. Since the independent variables are related to the urban structure: population of zone declines with distance from centre, and income level increases; shifts in the form of the relationship altering the effect of the individual variables reflect changes in location of establishments within the structure--for instance, the decentralization pattern.

For further information the regression relations between stores, sales, and the factor scores of consumer characteristics may be examined. These results are not comparable since different factors emerged at the two different time periods, yet they demonstrate the continued relevance of the consumer-commercial relationship: The more complex model provides much better prediction.

TABLE 18

RESIDUALS FROM REGRESSION

(Expressed in Per Cent of Observed-- $\frac{O-E}{O}$)

Zone		1951			1961			Ground Floor Vacancy Rate (1964)
		Stores[a]	Sales[b]	Sales/ Store	Stores[c]	Sales[d]	Sales/ Store	
I	Central	18.7	23.5	61,900	28.0	41.9	93,100	7.9
II	West End	9.1	- 6.5	52,700	7.9	- 10.3	66,700	7.0
III	East End	- 10.9	- 4.7	66,200	- 4.3	- 5.9	81,900	6.5
IV	Uptown	- 6.8	6.8	83,300	16.4	18.4	109,600	3.8
V	Lakeshore	0.2	9.5	72,300	- 2.0	6.3	117,000	5.4
VI	Northwest	- 9.8	0.4	66,100	-18.7	- 21.6	79,200	5.5
VII	Scarboro S.	- 89.4	- 71.5	68,600	-11.7	- 8.1	110,800	5.5
VIII	Etobicoke	80.2	10.2	99,300	- 4.4	3.6	141,100	3.5
IX	N. York	- 80.3	- 45.6	87,600	-54.8	- 4.1	140,100	6.0
X	Bayview	146.8	16.9	85,600	49.2	- 14.8	181,100	4.1
XI	Scarboro N.	-122.0	-125.4	54,100	-36.2	- 31.3	128,900	4.4
XII	Far West	......	......	......	34.6	- 0.3	101,400	6.4
XIII	Far North	......	......	......	- 9.9	- 19.2	86,500	4.2
XIV	Far East	......	......	......	-80.5	-163.0	68,000	6.5

[a]Establishments = 1341 + 0.01328 Population - 0.4966 Income (r^2 = 0.96)
   (0.00110)   (0.1943)

[b]Sales = 29280 + 0.8348 Population - 10.80 Income (r^2 = 0.97)
   (0.0582)   (10.31)

[c]Establishments = 1190 + 0.01329 Population - 0.3080 Income (r^2 = 0.89)
   (0.00154)   (0.0940)

[d]Sales = 24150 + 1.059 Population - 4.033 Income (r^2 = 0.83)
   (0.149)   (9.069)

	Popu-lation	I	II	III	IV	V
(4.14) 1951[1] E =	30.72 +	0.00312 +	0.4735 +	0.3758 +	1.111	−0.5687 −0.1076
		(0.00047)	(0.3117)	(0.4936)	(0.3206)	(0.4245) (0.3404)

$$(r^2 = 0.989)$$

(4.15) S =	3211 +	0.04782	−21.63 +	47.79 +	20.36 +	0.1842 + 6.923
		(0.00473)	(3.150)	(4.988)	(3.240)	(4.290) (3.440)

$$(r^2 = 0.998)$$

	Popu-ulation	I	II	III	IV	V	VI	VII
(4.16) 1961 E =	566	+0.00849	+1.58	−2.63	−3.52	−2.84	+3.99	+1.46 +5.64
		(0.00202)	(0.75)	(0.76)	(0.95)	(1.56)	(1.53)	(0.74) (2.48)

$$(r^2 = 0.993)$$

(4.17) S =	13566	+1.039	−197.	−321.	−349.	+98.3	−192	+30.4 −166.
		(0.31)	(115)	(117)	(146)	(240)	(236)	(115) (382)

$$(r^2 = 0.969)$$

The patterns of explanation are complex and changing over time. Sales are more closely tied to the socio-economic (I) and family structure (II) factors than stores. The ethnic variable (III) is more effective in 1951 than ethnic factors IV and VI in 1961, when the amenity factor (III) is quite powerful instead.

Shifts Among Business Types

As the consumer becomes older or wealthier he spends his money in different ways, and as new retailing techniques emerge some forms of retailing flourish while others decline. Even when there is little change in the total number of stores in an area the shifts among the business types may create surpluses of certain kinds of facilities. Table 19 indicates the degree and direction of change in Toronto. Since the city, as the oldest part of the metropolitan area, reflects the greatest lag between retail and service facilities and the consumer's needs, it may be assumed that this table understates the total change in the system. Unfortunately, data for the larger region is not available in this detail.

Despite the 1.7 per cent per annum increase in real income and the continued growth of its trading area population, the number of establishments in the city has remained relatively constant. Economies of scale which resulted

---

[1]The factors for 1951:
   I   Low socio-economic level
  II   Urban downtown
 III   Non-British origin
  IV   White-collar workers
   V   High-mobility, low-amenity

TABLE 19

CHANGING NUMBER OF ESTABLISHMENTS BY BUSINESS TYPE[1]
City of Toronto

	1930	1941	1951	1961
Food	(3605)	(3969)	3388	(3268)
Candy	478	418	276	(254)
Groceries	1581	1414	1228	1027
Meat and Fish	357	378	260	(298)
Restaurants	630	957	1057	(1150)
General	185	192	230	134
Variety Stores	30	63	66	91
Automotive	588	757	625	(701)
Dealers	95	126	170	144
Garages	105	105	63	(73)
Service Stations	310	446	327	364
Apparel	1357	1601	1703	1631
Men's Wear	427	415	549	(504)
Women's Wear	645	892	796	(751)
Family Clothing	95	109	86	153
Shoes	190	185	210	253
Building Materials and Hardware	345	313	367	(357)
Lumber	22	26	41	(40)
Hardware	208	190	210	212
Furniture	257	308	442	(466)
Furniture	57	74	104	165
Household Appliances	129	132	227	(165)
Second Hand	273	238	144	(81)
Other Retail	(2112)	(2018)	1810	(1798)
Drugs	398	443	448	346
Tobacco	560	721	559	(554)
Jewellery	98	107	185	186
TOTAL RETAIL	8725	9396	8709	(8436)
Per Cent of Total	72.2	68.3	70.0	64.7
Amusements	210	259	259	(256)
Theatres	92	102	115	(74)
Business Services	109	284	368	(589)
Personal Services	1714	2509	2205	(2564)
Beauty and Barber	887	1210	879	1227
Shoe Repair	70	507	321	291
Repair Services	874	743	601	(626)
Automobile	244	280	313	(326)
Undertaking	62	62	48	39
Photographers	82	112	110	153
Hotels	40	127	46	46

TABLE 19--Continued

	1930	1941	1951	1961
Miscellaneous	415	294	85	(363)
TOTAL SERVICES	3356	4390	3722	(4636)
Per Cent of Total	27.8	31.7	30.0	35.3
GRAND TOTAL	12,081	13,786	12,431	(13,072)

[1]Data derived from Dominion Bureau of Statistics, Census of Canada, 1931, 1941, 1951, and 1961. Due to major changes in the census categories in the period 1951-61, exact numbers of establishments in 1961 under the earlier definitions required estimation techniques, denoted by the parentheses surrounding the estimate.

from technological and economic achievement make it profitable to build larger stores rather than more stores (refer to Table 17 for changing store size). There is a general trend toward increased numbers of service establishments and slightly fewer retail stores, the latter being more suitable to scale economies. The greatest part of the variation in number of establishments derives from the services, particularly personal services, which have an uneven career. It is difficult to predict these variations since each business type responds differently, depending on the nature of its production function, the relevance of technological change, and the personal preferences of the consumer.

Frictional Blight

The final aspect of blight to be considered results from the interaction of different land uses. In the next chapter we will consider the impact of commercial areas on other land uses; here we define frictional blight as the blighting of commercial facilities by other types of land use. Considerable disagreement exists in the planning literature as to whether a mixture of land uses is necessarily bad, or bad only under certain conditions.[1] Evidence from this study indicates that certain combinations of commercial and industrial land use form a very effective symbiosis; for instance, service stations and restaurants which serve factory workers, and the clothes stores and clothing factories of the garment district. Yet quite often the traffic generated by industrial and wholesaling land uses, as well as the noise and general unattractiveness of these activities can contribute to the blighting of commercial establishments. Most of the points raised in this discussion could also be applied to conflicts between different categories of commercial use.

In order to explore the extent of this problem Figure 16 was drafted, based on the field survey. It identifies blocks within the study area which are shared by a manufacturing or wholesale land use and at least four commercial establishments. The latter number was chosen first, because the field data ignored smaller aggregations, and secondly, it seemed to focus on the more serious areas of conflict, avoiding the restaurant-gas station situation mentioned above.

Note that the important areas of frictional blight are much more concentrated than the total distribution of commercial facilities (Figure 4). The worst area is south and west of College and University extending to Queen, with two other strips: one out Weston Road; the other on Dundas West. The other occurrences are scattered widely throughout the metropolitan area. Like the maps of deteriorated (Figure 11) and vacant (Figure 13) stores, friction is most intense in Zones I, II, and III but there is too much variation in the patterns to be able to say they are closely related.

These major areas of land use friction may be considered as symptomatic of problems in the commercial structure. A healthy commercial area can easily

---

[1]For instance, Webster, Urban Planning and Municipal Public Policy, p. 148, "Compatability in land uses is also important. As a general rule, a combination of stores and residences is undesirable. Such a combination tends to create parking problems and makes for poor residential environment, particularly for children. However, the location of apartment houses as a part of such areas may be consistent with the planned use of the district," represents the one point of view, but increasingly, the attitude is changing; see the Royal Architectural Institute of Canada, Reflection on Zoning (Ottawa, 1963), p. 13, ". . . the result of the newer kind of zoning is that larger and larger areas of exclusively residential environment has produced a monotony of environment that some people now feel is as unacceptable as was the earlier mixed environment. We think that the 'residential environment' can be made more attractive for all residents by a more discriminate mixture of land use and housing types" and p. 17, "We could see no reason why apartments could not be constructed over some of our new shopping centres and possibly at a reduced cost."

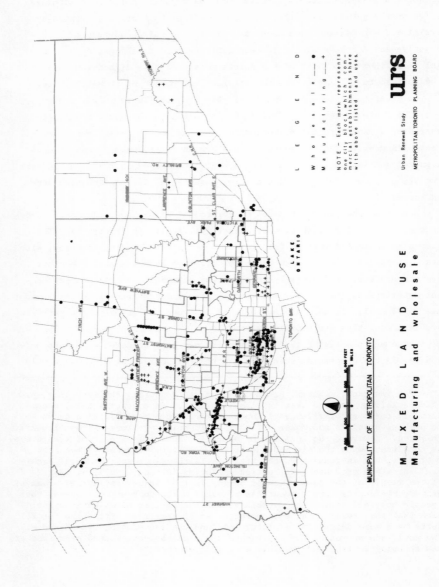

Fig. 16.—Mixed Land Use—Wholesaling and Manufacturing

outbid other uses for the location it desires. The presence of manufacturing and wholesalers in a commercial zone encourages functional blight by hampering the adjustment to larger size, better parking, and a wider trade area; and making the rehabilitation of these areas more difficult.

CHAPTER IV

RENEWAL

The Distribution of Blight in Toronto

Throughout this study we have identified four forms of commercial blight. The distribution patterns of their respective symptoms: deterioration (physical), vacancy rates (economic and functional) and mixed land use (frictional), confirm the hypothesis that these blight forms stem from different causes and will require different kinds of renewal treatment. Figure 17 combines the distributions of these phenomena on one map which reveals their general independence, but shows some areas of overlap where all forms of blight must be combatted.[1] Deterioration is concentrated near the Central Area on both the east and west sides in the older part of the city, with extensions along the early roads, particularly to the east, and scattered occurrences in older outlying commercial areas. High vacancy rates are also found in the older parts of the city with some occurrences in suburban areas where temporary over-building has taken place. Mixed land use is related to transportation routes which were attractive sites for industry and wholesaling; for example, Dundas and Weston Road. There is also a large area of frictional blight centering on Spadina and Queens, the garment manufacturing and wholesaling district.

Areas which suffer from the whole range of commercial blight and hence are particularly important for renewal are also defined on the map:

Area One--Queen and Spadina, includes a number of specialized activities: the Garment district, Kensington Market, University-oriented services, and antique stores, each of which will require special renewal consideration.

Area Two--The area around Queen Street and Dovercourt Road exhibits all forms of commercial blight. It is surrounded by a declining residential population which has problems of its own as evidenced by three city urban renewal areas nearby. Queen Street is dominated by bargain stores and second-hand stores but there is no real commercial focus. The stores exist independently, mixed with manufacturing uses.

---

[1]The break points used to delimit this map are quite arbitrary. The vacancy and deterioration rates chosen delimit about 20 per cent of the tracts, 50 out of 235 and 42 out of 234 respectively. Only 19 of 296 tracts were deemed to have sufficiently serious problems of frictional blight.

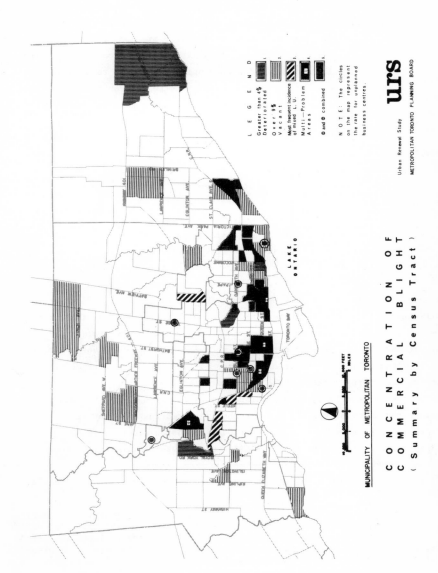

Fig. 17.--Concentrations of Commercial Blight

Area Three—Queen Street East, around Broadview, has similar characteristics although the population is more stable. The city's
Riverdale renewal scheme plans a reduction in commercial
zoning and a greater degree of concentration of stores.[1]

Area Four—Eglinton and Weston Road, although much farther from the
city centre, rates consistently high on all blight
criteria. Although this is in a low-income section with
slightly declining population it appears to be stable and
well kept. A major problem is the discontinuity and mixing
of land use in an area broken up by physical barriers,
railways, and major streets.

All four districts are imbedded in a wide "gray area"[2] stretching in a
crescent from Weston to Victoria Park Road and containing the major concentration of each kinds of blight as well as most of the marginally blighted
districts. This crescent consists of the two main low-income sectors of the
city and has undergone very little population growth.

The gray area contrasts strongly with the absence of blight phenomena
in the long established commercial area along Yonge north of Bloor, extending
to the city limits. With the exception of six deteriorated structures at
Yonge-Castlefield, there are few problems in the eight unplanned centres and
1500 ribbon establishments of Zone IV. The ground floor vacancy rate is 3.8
per cent; the upper floor 10.0 per cent. The construction of offices and
apartments in this area is increasing the population and lifting the income
level while clearing away older commercial structures in the process. In this
zone, renewal by the private sector has more than kept up with obsolescence.

There is little evidence of commercial blight in the portion of the
planning area outside Metro. The few deteriorated structures in the outlying
centres should quickly disappear during the rapid expansion of the next decade.
Although the study of the Chicago suburbs indicated that the new retail structure based on planned centres made serious inroads on older unplanned centres,
this is unlikely to happen to the small centres outside Toronto.[3] These

---

[1]City of Toronto Planning Board, Improvement Program for Residential
Areas (1965).

[2]The term gray areas was coined by Raymond Vernon, Anatomy of a Metropolis (Cambridge: Harvard University Press, 1960) to describe vast residential
areas of New York City which are beset by problems similar to those indicated
here, i.e., limited amounts of physical and economic blight, with widespread
obsolescence due to a rapidly changing environment.

[3]Berry and Tennant, Metropolitan Planning Guidelines—Commercial Structure, Chapter III.

centres do not depend greatly on shopping goods activities which are highly
susceptible to new competition. The population growth will be more than ade-
quate to maintain the low order goods and services which are found there.

Relation to Residential Blight

The Urban Renewal Studies

Before discussing the implications of our investigation for renewal
planning, we shall briefly examine the interaction of commercial blight and
residential blight. During the period of the commercial study the Metro
Toronto Urban Renewal Study made two separate surveys of residential blight.
First, after outlining all the possible blight areas designated by earlier
studies, they did a windshield survey of structural deterioration using the
criteria discussed in Chapter II. Figure 18 shows that the areas designated
for blight investigation cover the same crescent as the commercial blight.

The second approach to the identification of residential blight was the
special census analysis discussed in Appendix D. Using census tract observations and the full range of census measurements, two factors indicating blight
emerged. Factor one measures socio-economic achievement which varies in a
series of sectors around the central area. The two major low-income sectors,
to the east and to the northwest (Figure 19) define major concentrations of all
types of commercial blight. A low score on the other factor (III) indicates a
lack of important household amenities such as furnace, flush toilet, bath, and
refrigeration, and correlates closely with commercial deterioration. Both
these forms of blight stem from the same causes of age and low-incomes.

The more detailed analysis of housing data by enumeration area demonstrated that residential blight is also complex, with at least three independent
dimensions: old, deteriorated high density areas; older housing with shared
plumbing facilities; and low value housing with no bath, furnace, or running
water. Like the commercial blight characteristics they occur within the same
broad crescent but with considerable individual variation.

Friction Between Commercial
and Residential Uses

Despite the degree of similarity in the causes and distributions of
residential and commercial blight, it is difficult to identify the relationship
between commercial and residential decay precisely. The most obvious effect of
commercial blight is the visual impact of deteriorated or vacant stores which,
by their prominent location, set the tone for the residential area. Inadequate

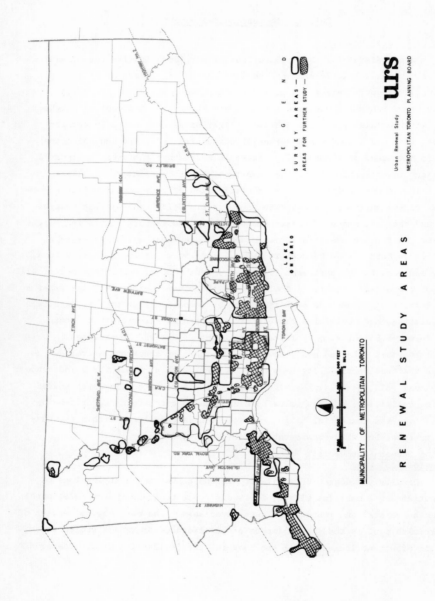

Fig. 18.--Renewal Study Areas

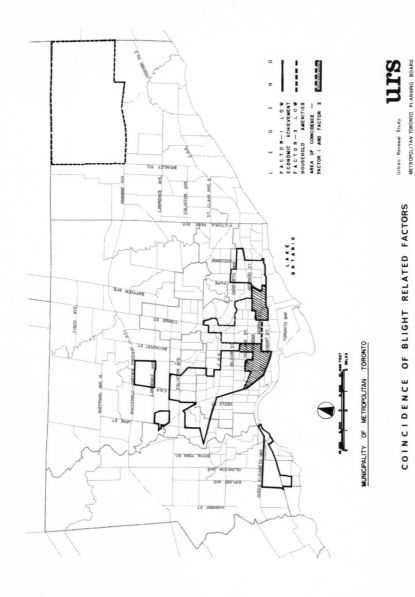

MUNICIPALITY OF METROPOLITAN TORONTO

COINCIDENCE OF BLIGHT RELATED FACTORS

Urban Renewal Study
METROPOLITAN TORONTO PLANNING BOARD

Fig. 19.--Coincidence of Blight-Related Factors

commercial facilities may create traffic, fire, or policing hazards which
spread into the surrounding neighborhoods. Two maps were prepared from the
field survey data in order to try to evaluate interaction and possible frictions
between the land uses. The implications of mixed land use are beyond the com-
petence of this study since, as pointed out earlier, it is controversial even
among professional planners. In a renewal program, land use friction will be
evaluated for each individual area.

Figure 20 records the location of blocks in which residences are found
among at least four commercial establishments, i.e., stores at both ends of the
block. 'It is a widespread combination, found wherever commercial establishments exist. Particularly prominent are the main commercial arteries: both the
old--Bloor, Dundas, Weston Road, St. Clair, Kingston Road; and the more recent--
Wilson Avenue and the Queensway. Also plotted on this map are stores converted
to residential use, an unattractive and undesirable occurrence in any residential area. The pattern correlates with commercial deterioration, suggesting
that the conversions are a result of physical decay rather than a result of
surplus commercial facilities.

The next map, Figure 21, shows the per cent of stores having occupied
residential units on the upper floors. The pattern is doughnut-shaped, with
highest ratio in the middle zone. Toward the city centre the upper floors are
used for offices and services, and in the newer commercial areas the trend is
toward separation of commercial and residential buildings. High income sectors
have a lower ratio of residences over stores because the market for such accom-
modations is reduced.

Urban Renewal and Commercial Blight

A program of urban renewal must be at least as complex as the blight
which it is designed to eradicate. We may expect the renewal of commercial
areas to require different procedures for each of the different kinds of problems, but urban renewal is an increasingly complex concept in itself,

81

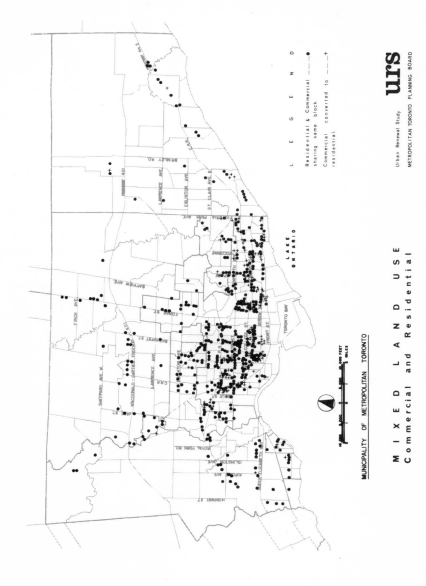

Fig. 20.—Mixed Land Use—Commercial and Residential

82

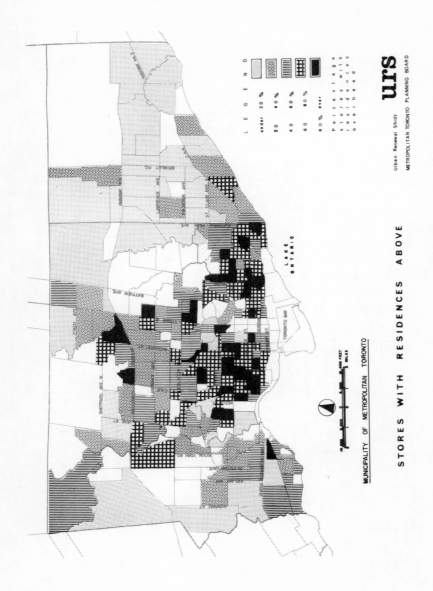

MUNICIPALITY OF METROPOLITAN TORONTO

STORES WITH RESIDENCES ABOVE

Urban Renewal Study

METROPOLITAN TORONTO PLANNING BOARD

Fig. 21.--Stores with Residences Above

particularly as we become more experienced in its use.[1] Three main issues must
be decided in undertaking a specific program: first, what is the frame of
reference? For which group of people are the benefits maximized--the people of
the area or the community as a whole, the tenants or the taxpayers, etc.? The
second problem concerns the size of the area to be treated. Do you use less
intensive measures, conservation or rehabilitation techniques, over a wide area
where many of the structures are still useful, or do you concentrate on more
drastic action in a small area? Finally, there is the question of the time
scale. Should the program be a short-term adjustment, a more permanent redevelopment, or a program of long-time adjustment to change? The answers to
these questions vary with the area and the type of blight under consideration.

Most renewal concepts have been derived from the analysis of residential blight, but a program of commercial renewal may introduce different
constraints. Rightly or wrongly, planning and renewal programs have not been
concerned with improving the economic condition of the individual entrepreneur.
Although a community may repair or replace a residential structure to improve
the lot of the inhabitants, the same criteria are not used for commercial areas
where, by and large, merchants are allowed to fail or succeed on their own.[2]
Commercial areas are renewed because either (a) they blight nearby residential
areas, or (b) the community requires the land for some other purpose, possibly
with a higher tax return.

The replacement of cleared facilities is a much more important problem
for commercial areas. The market for residential facilities is generally
assured, given a reasonable price level, but there is often a surplus of stores
in renewal areas. Retailing is such a fast changing business that any rebuilding or rehabilitation must be undertaken with caution and with full knowledge
of trends in demand and supply.

---

[1]Urban renewal from the point of view of the Metropolitan Toronto Urban
Renewal Study is discussed in detail in the "Interim Report" (February, 1965),
p. 49. Some excellent examples of current urban renewal discussion are Max R.
Bloom, "Fiscal Productivity and the Pure Theory of Urban Renewal," Land
Economics, XXXVIII (May, 1962), pp. 134-144; George S. Duggar, "Urban Renewal:
Current Criticism and the Search for a Rationale," Public Management (September,
1962); Claude Gruen,"Urban Renewal's Role in the Genesis of Tomorrow's Slums,"
Land Economics, XXXIX (August, 1963), pp. 285-291; and Peter Morris, "Report on
Urban Renewal," Journal of the American Institute of Planners, XXVIII (May,
1962), pp. 180-186.

[2]The exception has been the relocation and reconstruction of produce
markets in several cities, but these activities have long been considered a
municipal responsibility. I would also exclude cases where commercial facilities are constructed as a service to the residential population.

With these constraints in mind, Table 20 summarizes the range of blight symptoms, causes, and renewal solutions. Each type of blight may be discussed in detail, but the effects of their interaction should not be ignored.[1] There is evidence that the vacancies which originate from economic or functional blight eventually show up in any deteriorated structures which may exist in the vicinity, simplifying the renewal procedure. Some of the effects of frictional blight are similar to obsolescence, e.g., constraints on adaptation to new requirements. Most closely related are economic and functional blight. Although there are no areas of economic blight in Toronto in the sense of serious decline in population and income level, obsolescence is a serious problem in stable areas. Only those older areas where population and income are increasing are able to attract the new investment necessary to avoid functional blight.

Physical Blight

Deteriorated structures are the first thing that comes to mind when discussing commercial blight. Yet, at present, this is not a serious problem. There are only 355 stores in this condition out of a total of 22,500, about 1.6 per cent. Twenty-five per cent of these buildings are vacant and most of the rest are occupied by small, low-order service and retailing establishments. Many of the deteriorated stores in outlying areas will soon disappear as the city continues to grow, but there are about 300 establishments in this condition in the older zones. Given the severe definition of deterioration used by the field study, the only solution is removal. Since these are also zones of high vacancy rates, there need be no problem of replacement.

Physical blight will be an increasing problem in the future, however. Each decade brings greater numbers of buildings to the age of decay. In the long run, these stores must be eliminated in as many ways and as efficiently as possible, perhaps as part of the growth and expansion of the city. The future problem area lies in the crescent where economic and functional blight are also serious, creating surpluses of commercial facilities. The most painful loss will be that of the small merchants who can operate only under marginal conditions. Zimmer's study indicates that these store owners are not successful subjects for relocation.[2]

---

[1] There is a thorough discussion of the relationship between blight forms in Berry, _Commercial Structure and Commercial Blight_, p. 197ff.

[2] Zimmer, _Rebuilding Cities_, is a very thorough study of the relocation of merchants displaced by urban renewal projects. The stores concerned are usually small, low gross, businesses run by older, poorly educated, proprietors who live nearby.

TABLE 20

RENEWAL OF COMMERCIAL BLIGHT

	Symptoms	Cause	Remedy
A. Physical	- deteriorated buildings - conversion to residential use	- age, - plus factors B, C, D which discourage new investment	- removal (plenty of alternate sites)
B. Economic	- vacancies - decline in population and income	- decline in demand or increase in supply - specific vacancies will be determined by the other forms of blight	- growth areas will catch up - non-growth areas require removal or specific form of rehabilitation--e.g., reduction in number of stores by increasing size
C. Functional	- vacancies - high ratio of stores per population unit - high proportion urban arterial - outdated mix of stores - dispersion of commercial activities toward newer parts of the city	- demographic shifts - higher incomes - increased mobility - technological innovation - different consumer demands	- acceptance - removal - assistance in renovation and adjustment (rehabilitation) - anticipation of obsolescence
D. Frictional	- commercial uses next to manufacturing and wholesaling	- inadequate zoning - misunderstanding of interaction between uses	- spot removal - rationalization of whole land use mix

Economic Blight

      Vacancies resulting from decline in population or income level are not
widespread in Metro Toronto. The expansion of the immigrant areas of the west
end has not been accompanied by significant decrease in income. In fact, these
areas have had an increase in number of stores. However, as pointed out
earlier, stability in the income level of an area is not sufficient to overcome
the effects of obsolescence. In the absence of growth a new discount centre, a
planned centre farther out, or the ribbon independent stores with good parking
will displace many of the local merchants. This process is best observed in
the eastern part of the city along Gerrard Street and around the Queen-Lee
centre. In a growth area the older facilities would be needed and there would
be capital available to rehabilitate and bring them up to the new standards.
The problem then, is primarily a form of functional blight.

Functional Blight

      By far the most serious problem facing the commercial structure of
Metropolitan Toronto is functional obsolescence--buildings which are badly
located; inadequate in scale; lacking various specialized facilites such as air
conditioning, lighting, storage space, etc.; and with inadequate parking. It
is a complaint common to every North American city, as has frequently been
pointed out.[1] In Toronto, functional blight is responsible for most of the
1500 commercial vacancies and contributes to the distribution of deterioration
and frictional blight in the gray area. Zones of analysis I, II, and II, in
this area, have the highest vacancy rates (6.8 per cent), highest deterioration
rates (2.4 per cent) and the majority of the land-use friction problems.

      It must be recognized that the main causal factors--higher incomes,
increased mobility, demographic shifts, and the outward dispersal of retail
facilities are largely irreversible.[2] Adjustment rather than replacement is
required. This point is underlined when the scale of the functional blight
problem is considered. The three zones threatened by functional blight include
thirteen unplanned centres and over 6,000 stores. Not all of these stores are
inadequate in themselves, but they may be poorly located or grouped in inadequate aggregations. If the irreversibility of functional blight is accepted, a

---

[1] Berry, Commercial Structure and Commercial Blight, p. 163.

[2] The irreversibility of the trends affecting the retail structure are
convincingly demonstrated by George Sternlieb, "The Future of Retailing in the
Downtown Core," Journal of the American Institute of Planners, XXIX (May, 1963),
pp. 102-112.

renewal program must encourage the continued removal of stores in the problem areas. To this end more precise models linking supply and demand of facilities will be required (see the section to follow).

A more positive program would encourage merchants and merchant groups in these areas, by means of technical assistance and loans, to renovate, to modernize, and to tackle traffic and parking problems. Such a program must include research to try and anticipate the future requirements of retailing: the variation in demand characteristics--income, family size, customer requirements; and the direction of change in the supply side--scale of operations, specialization, and interaction between business types.

Although much of the commercial obsolescence now visible is a result of the introduction of the family car into areas designed prior to 1930, the new retail structure which is emerging has a serious form of obsolescence built into it. The problem results from the nature of planned centres, which are built as units with a mix of stores, store size, lay-out, and location dependent on their scale or level in the retail hierarchy.[1] As a result, these shopping centres cannot adjust their size upward or downward in response to feedback from the consumer or from their competition. Any change in the commercial structure requires the addition or deletion of a centre, involving sudden changes of several hundred thousand square feet of floor space. The results of this change are illustrated by a current controversy in the Toronto area. The recent application for an amendment to a local official plan to allow the construction of a super-regional level shopping centre on the west side of Toronto (Sherway) was strongly opposed by the management of three nearby regional shopping plazas and the municipality in which the nearest unplanned centre is located. Although the site may be quite appropriate and viable for its projected purpose and brings certain benefits to consumers, it will subject nearby centres to severe economic blight--produced this time by a sudden increase in supply rather than a decline in demand. There appears to be no way to insert a centre of this scale into the existing system without blighting the nearby centres.

As the planned centre component of the commercial structure continues to expand, problems of this sort will increase. Decisions about transportation routes, for instance, will have dramatic effects on centres of this sort, as will zoning and other planning decisions. There are various solutions to this problem, none of them entirely satisfactory. It has been suggested that the

---

[1]Simmons, The Changing Pattern of Retail Location, p. 105.

municipality guarantee a centre freedom from competition for a fixed period of time, by refusing to re-zone the surrounding area.[1] Although this might relieve the distress of the developer in the short-run, ultimately the community will be faced with the problem of surplus facilities. Horwood recommends that the location of new planned centres require a public hearing like a public utility or a new broadcasting station, with various points of view presented and evaluation based on both economic and planning criteria.[2] The hearing which took place in the case cited above was a step in this direction, although no criteria have yet been established for making decisions. The procedure must be accompanied by continuing studies into the nature of an optimal retail structure, so that we can intelligently weigh the costs of inadequate commercial facilities at present against the future costs of commercial blight. In the next section the discussion on retail models will present some suggestions in this regard.

Frictional Blight

The interaction of commercial with industrial and wholesaling activities is concentrated in a relatively small area. However, any one such incidence may mean a whole block of stores blighted by traffic and noise. As was pointed out earlier healthy commercial areas should be able to overcome such activities by out-bidding them in the market: serious problems emerge only in areas where other blight forms create vacancies or lower store rents.

Mixed land use is the problem at which most planning techniques are currently aimed. It can only be pointed out that there will be increasing possibilities of admixtures of commercial and other uses in the newer forms of urban arterial ribbons. There we have stores dependent primarily on automobile driving customers, requiring large amounts of parking space, and with little interaction between stores. Commercial activities of this sort are less able to dominate land values than in more traditional retailing areas, so that retail, industrial and wholesaling uses are more likely to locate side by side.

---

[1]Conversations with my colleagues Professor E. G. Pleva and G. M. Adler of the University of Western Ontario.

[2]Edgar M. Horwood, "Public Policy and the Outlying Shopping Center," Journal of the American Institute of Planners, XXIV (November, 1958), pp. 215-222.

Anticipating Future Blight

In his study of commercial blight in the Chicago suburbs Berry defines three levels of renewal planning:[1]

short-run programs use the existing relationships between supply and demand factors to remove existing blight. Clearance and rehabilitation are the tools.

long-run renewal plans anticipate future obsolescence by projecting future changes in the parameters of the relations due to shifts in technology and consumer behavior. Once the optimal structure for a future point in time is predicted, the whole range of planning techniques may be used to attain that end.

long-term ("perspective") planning involves wide open speculation on the nature of the future city, its population and the commercial facilities required to serve it. These predictions will guide the nature and location of commercial facilities still unbuilt.

The Utility of the Toronto Study

This study was primarily aimed toward short-run proposals. By defining the present equilibrium structure we have been able to identify blighted elements, resulting in suggestions for removal or rehabilitation to adjust the structure to the present-day conditions. It is at the middle level of long-run programming where the most useful work remains to be done. Although the factors causing obsolescence and the nature of their effects have been indicated in this study, there is a need for much more detailed study of changing demand and supply factors in order to offset future demands by examining the mix of incomes and family structure and determining the basket of goods which will be required. Changing patterns of consumer travel should be studied since there are indications that average trip length, number of centres visited, and the distribution of the shopping dollar among different levels of centres and types of stores are shifting rapidly. Most important, especially with regard to any program of replacement of commercial facilities, is study into the nature of supply characteristics of commercial facilities (particularly the trend to increasing sales and floor areas for individual stores). Table 17 indicates that the average annual increase in real sales per store in Metro Toronto is 2.1 per cent, and Table 18 shows that new areas average over twice

---

[1] Berry and Tennant, Metropolitan Planning Guidelines: Commercial Structure, p. 40.

the sales per store of the older zones. This increase in scale will absorb much of the effect of income increases over time. When equations 4.7 and 4.8 were applied to a typical stable zone, the changes which produced a sales increase of over 8 per cent resulted in only 1 per cent increase in number of stores.

The present study provides a good base for long-run renewal planning and renewal by defining the present structure including the centres, the mix of stores in each type of aggregation and the basic relations with the customer. Using only these data, it is possible to simulate the effect of retail decisions in the near future such as addition or removal of certain store groups. A repeat of the field study in five to ten years would define precisely the nature of obsolescence: which locations and aggregations were most severely affected; which store types are threatened; and the pattern of dispersal of retail facilities.

The equations relating stores, sales and population characteristics may also be used for long-term planning. Although the simple models which used population and income as independent variables was rather rough, as shown by the size of the residuals in Table 18, the more complex model which used factor scores produced very accurate predictions. The factor scores are difficult to project in time, but some compromise between these models could be devised, with more attainable variables used to represent family structure, etc. Also worth exploring is the use of different areal units for analysis, perhaps proper ecological units. For low-order activities the zones used in this study are too coarse, obscuring the effects of local population changes, while certain specialized high order goods should be analyzed on a metropolitan-wide basis.

It is also necessary to predict the changes in the parameters of the equations. By extending the comparisons provided by equations 4.9 to 4.14 over time it is possible to foretell the direction and degree of parameter shifts.[1] Although, as Berry points out,[2] shifts in parameters tend to be "lumpy" because of the abrupt change from unplanned to planned systems, we are able to evaluate the sudden changes because we have parameters from both systems, as listed in equations 4.1 to 4.4.

---

[1] Simmons, The Changing Pattern of Retail Location, pp. 162-163, discusses the changing parameters of a number of retail relationships.

[2] Brian J. L. Berry, "The Retail Component of the Urban Model," Journal of the American Institute of Planners, XXXI (May, 1965), p. 151.

Models of Commercial Structure

Effective long-term planning will also require the use of more sophisticated models than those used here. The relatively simple concepts of hierarchy and consumer-store regressions may be complemented by the numerous retail models designed for prediction and renewal in other metropolitan areas.[1] Each of the models discussed below has been evaluated using real data.

The first two models, by Berry[2] and Lakshmanan and Hansen[3] are concerned primarily with retail centres--the high order component of the retail structure. These are only a small part of the commercial structure in Toronto but a small number of centre location decisions will shape the whole retail structure in the years to come. Berry's model is derived from the work on the Chicago Metropolitan area and relates the characteristics of a centre to the characteristics of the trade area assigned to it, by a series of regression relationships. Prediction for renewal planning is obtained by altering the trade area charactistics in order to observe the effect on the centres. The Lakshmanan-Hansen model, prepared for the Baltimore Metropolitan Area, assumes overlapping trade areas, with each centre attracting customers from all parts of the city--proportional to the size of centre and its distance from the residential area. The most interesting contribution of this model is the use of criteria for evaluating the best set of centres in a given area (the crux of the Sherway problem). Constraints on centre size, minimum sales per square foot in a centre, average trip length, and sales per square foot for a given region, are used to optimize this system.

The models by Lowry[4] and Harris[5] are more general. The former generates retail space and employment in a given area using a trip generation model in

---

[1]The definitive statement on urban model-building is the recent issue of the Journal of the American Institute of Planners, "Urban Development Models: New Tools for Planning," XXXI (May, 1965). An overview of the model-building process is provided by Ira S. Lowry, "A Short Course in Model Design," Journal of the American Institute of Planners, XXXI (May, 1965), pp. 158-166.

[2]Berry, "The Retail Component of the Urban Model."

[3]T. R. Lakshmanan and W. G. Hansen, "A Retail Market Potential Model," Journal of the American Institute of Planners, XXXI (May, 1965), pp. 134-143.

[4]Ira S. Lowry, A Model of Metropolis (Santa Monica: Rand Corporation, 1964), RM 4035-RC.

[5]Britton Harris, "A Model of Locational Equilibrium for Retail Trade," (Philadelphia: Penn-Jersey Transportation Study, 1964), mimeo.

which the drawing power of commercial facilities declines with distance; constrained by industrial and residential land use distributions, residential density restrictions, and retail thresholds. Each variable is linked to one or more of the others and proceeds from a given initial distribution by a series of iterations until a final equilibrium is attained. Harris' model is more directly concerned with retail facilities. He links the demand and supply of commercial space by a trip generation model similar to Lowry's which describes the consumer's propensity to travel and shop around. The initial supply of retail facilities is modified to meet the demand generated by the model in a series of iterations until a satisfactory equilibrium is attained.

Long-Term Planning

The fundamental changes in the commercial system must lead to some searching looks into the future if we are to prevent overly rapid obsolescence in the retail facilities currently being planned. Although growth and change accelerate obsolescence, they also provide an opportunity for adjustment and renewal during the normal processes of expansion and reconstruction. The onus is on the municipality to define its commitment to the incompatible interests of the entrepreneur, who wants zoning protection; the consumer, who is interested in the greatest possible variety of commercial facilities; and its own involvement in future urban renewal expenditures.

The types and locations of future high order centres will be an important problem. Will they be required to fit into a metropolitan-wide hierarchy and, if so, how will the system be determined? Or, since competition takes place primarily among different centres, should they be allowed to locate wherever they wish?

The proportion of establishments outside centres is not declining, and, in fact, planned centres lead to an increased number of ribbon establishments. In order to control the problem of mixed land use and traffic hazards, there is a need for innovations in their location. It may be possible to aggregate them into new kinds of planned centres, devoted not to shopping goods, but to urban arterial or specialized commercial activities. Conversion of existing planned centres made surplus by the expansion of the system may be an alternative solution. If there is a desire to concentrate commercial activities in a tight aggregation, the solution is not to restrict them to existing commercial districts, where existing land values and ownership patterns constrain the scale of new development, but to allow them to aggregate in larger integrated units in lower land value areas.

It is also necessary to look even farther into the future at forms of retailing still untested, although this is beyond the scope of our study. We have presented an overview of the present patterns of commercial blight in the Metropolitan Planning Area. In the process the existing commercial structure has been described as a basis for comparison with future studies, the degree of blight of different kinds was investigated and the worst problem areas designated. The rest is a matter for policy.

APPENDIX A--FIELD STUDY MATERIAL

COMMERCIAL INVENTORY CLASSIFICATION SHEET
(Refined to 4 digits from D.B.S. Standard Industrial Classification)

Name: _____

Type: _____

Food Stores
6310 Supermarkets
6311 Bake Shops
6312 Candy and confectionery stores
6313 Dairy products stores
6314 Delicatessen stores
6315 Fish markets
6316 Food stores, grocery & meat markets
6317 Fruit and vegetable markets
6318 Meat markets
6319 Food stores not elsewhere classified

General Merchandise Stores
6421 Department stores
6422 Mail order offices
6471 Discount stores
6472 Variety stores (chain)
6473 Variety stores
649- Other general merchandise stores not elsewhere classified

Retailers of Automotive Products
652- Automobile accessory, parts, tire & battery shops
6541 Gasoline service stations
6542 Car washing and polishing
6561 Motor vehicle dealers (new and used)
6562 Motor vehicle dealers (used only)
6581 Auto body work and painting
6582 Auto electric and ignition repair
6583 General auto repair
6589 Auto repair not elsewhere classified

Clothing and Shoe Stores
6631 Children's shoe stores
6632 Family shoe stores
6633 Men's shoe stores
6634 Women's shoe stores
6651 Men's clothing stores
6652 Men's furnishings
6671 Women's ready-to-wear stores
6672 Millinery shops
6673 Foundation garments, lingerie & hosiery shops
6674 Furriers and fur stores
6691 Children's clothing stores
6692 Family clothing stores
6693 Second-hand clothing stores
6694 Dry good stores
6699 Apparel & accessory shops not elsewhere classified

Hardware, Household Furniture & Appliance Stores
6731 Hardware stores
6732 Paint, glass, and wallpaper stores
6761 Antique shops
6762 Curtains and draperies
6763 Floor coverings
6764 Furniture stores
6765 Household appliance stores
6766 Radio & television stores
6767 Second-hand furniture
6769 Household furnishing stores not elsewhere classified
678- Radio, television, & electrical appliance repair shops

Other Retail Stores
681- Drug stores
6911 Book stores
6912 Stationery stores
692- Florists' shops
6931 Fuel oil & bottled gas dealers
6932 Other fuel dealers
694- Jewellery stores (incl. repairs)
6061 Beer stores
6962 Liquor stores
6963 Wine stores
697- Tobacconists
6981 Art galleries
6982 Bicycle shops
6983 Boats and marine supplies
6984 Cameras & photographic supplies
6985 Gift and novelty shops
6986 Hobby shops
6987 Luggage & leather goods stores
6988 Musical instruments stores
6989 Optical goods stores
6990 Pet stores
6991 Record stores
6992 Sporting goods dealers
6999 Retail stores not elsewhere classified

Finance, Insurance, and Real Estate
7021 Banks
7022 Finance and loan companies
7023 Mortgage companies
7024 Trust companies
7029 Savings and credit institutions not elsewhere classified
704- Investment companies & security dealers
731- Insurance agents and companies
735- Insurance and real estate agencies
737- Real estate operators

Community Services
8031 Commercial and business schools
8071 Libraries
809- Education & related services not elsewhere classified
821- Hospitals
823- Offices of physicians
825- Offices of dentists
8271 Offices of chiropractors
8272 Health & Welfare organizations
8273 Medical and dental laboratories
8274 Optometrists
8279 Health services not elsewhere classified
831- Religious organizations
851- Motion picture theatres
853- Bowling alleys and billiard parlours
859- Recreational facilities not elsewhere classified

Services to Business Management
861- Accountancy services
862- Advertising services
864- Engineering & scientific services
866- Legal services
8691 Blueprinting & duplicating services
8692 Employment agencies (not government)
8699 Business services not elsewhere classified

Personal Services
871- Shoe repair shops
8721 Barber shops
8722 Beauty shops
8741 Cleaning, dyeing and pressing
8742 Laundering service
8743 Laundromats
8744 Linen and uniform supply services
8745 Rug and carpet cleaning
8751 Taverns
8752 Restaurants
8753 Restaurants, drive-in
8754 Hotel, motor hotel
8755 Motel, motor court, tourist cabins
8756 Trailer courts and parks
876- Lodging houses & residential clubs
877- Funeral directors
8791 Clothing rental
8792 Dressmaking
8799 Personal services not elsewhere classified

Miscellaneous Services
891- Labour organizations & trade associations
893- Photography
894- Blacksmithing & welding shops
896- Repair shops not elsewhere classified
897- Services to buildings & dwellings
8991 Fraternal organizations
8992 Political organizations
8993 Automobile rentals
8994 Equipment rentals
8999 Miscellaneous services

V Vacant commercial structures
D Deteriorated commercial structures
NC New commercial construction not ready for occupancy
C Conversions of commercial structures to non-commercial uses
R Residential units
VR Vacant residential units in commercial structures
Vac Vacant land

SUMMARY FOR SHOPPING CENTERS & RIBBONS

	Ground Floor	Upper Floors	Total
No. of establishments			
No. of functions			
Vacancies			
Deteriorations			
Conversions to non-commercial uses			
Residential uses			

COMMENTS:

TABLE 21—COMMERCIAL INVENTORY CLASSIFICATION SHEET

TABLE 22

INDEX TO FIELD SHEETS

Organization

The field sheets are arranged in two forms:

1. individual streets (ribbon and scattered)
2. planned shopping centres

These are filed separately on the basis of location, in 11 districts which represent consolidations of municipal planning districts. (See location code.)

Coding Scheme

6310	= represents the classification of a commercial establishment employing a 4 digit modification of the DBS standard industrial classification (including 135 types of retail and service business)
R	= residential use
V	= vacant commercial
VR	= vacant residential
Vac.	= vacant land
D	= deteriorated commercial structure
NC	= new commercial construction
C	= conversion from commercial use
Whol.	= wholesale
Manuf. (Mfg.)	= manufacturing
off.	= office
R	= continuous residential use

Examples

6310/R	= a supermarket with residential use on the second floor
6310/R/R	= a supermarket with two floors of residential use above
6310/825-823-	= a supermarket with a doctor and a dentist on the second floor
6764/	= a furniture store covering 2 floors
Manuf////	= a manufacturing plant of 5 floors
R////	= a residential block of 5 floors
6764/825-x 2///R	= a furniture store with 2 dentists' offices on the second floor and three floors of residential above

TABLE 22--Continued

CR/R	= a commercial structure converted to residential use with one floor of residential above
8721/R D	= a barber shop with residential above, the structure is deteriorated
VD	= one storey commercial structure which is vacant and deteriorated
8721/R 8722/R 8741/R 6310/R 6316/R	= a planned commercial strip of 5 stores each with residential use above

6310/825-, 823-, 866-, 809 - is the same as $6310/\begin{matrix} 825 - \\ 823 - \\ 866 - \\ 809 - \end{matrix}$

Boundaries

orange (ochre) lines	- clusters and ribbons of commercial establishments

CT 297 CT 298 green lines	- census tracts

- - - - - - - -	- unplanned centres

Identification of Sheets

S.C.	- area location code (11 areas, representing consolidations of planning districts, i.e., South-Central)
Dundas St. W.	- street name
July 22 (18)	- date and page number for that street

Area Location Code

Symbol	Name	Planning Districts
C	Central	3, 4, 5
SC (1)*	South-central west	1, 2
SC (2)**	South-central east	6
NC	North-central	10, 11
WC	West-central	7, 8, 9
EC	East-central	12, 13, 14, 15, 16

TABLE 22--<u>Continued</u>

Symbol	Name	Planning Districts
N	North	20
NW	Northwest	19
NE	Northeast	21
W	West	17, 18
E	East	22, 23

*Excluding minor divisions "b" and "e" of District 1 (Central Business District) and division "c" and part of division "f" east of Yonge Street.

**Including division "c" and part of division "f" of District 1.

APPENDIX B--UNPLANNED AND PLANNED CENTRES

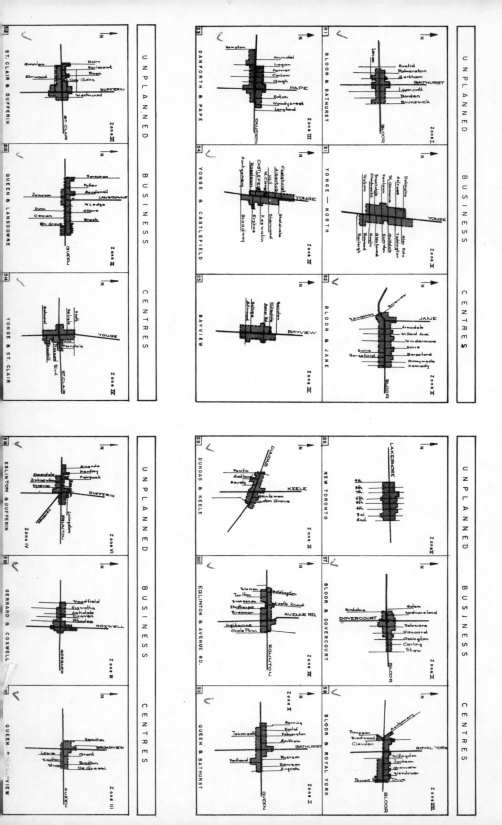

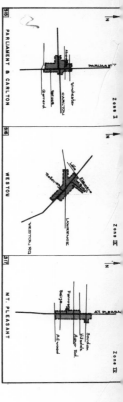

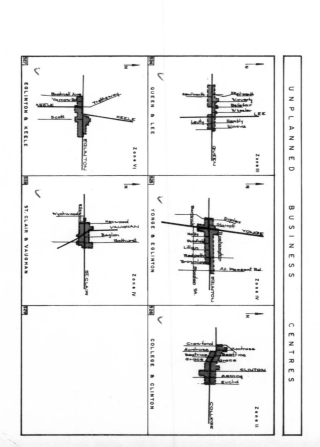

Fig. 22.—Unplanned Business Centres

100

TABLE 23

PLANNED CENTRES

Name	No.	Census Tract	Ground Floor Business Types	Number of Establishments		Per Cent Vacant	Number of Department Stores	Number of Chain Variety Stores	Number of Supermarkets
				Ground	Upper				
Yorkdale	SR1	220	45	77	0	18.0	2	1	1
Don Mills	R1	290	52	89	0	....	1	1	1
Cloverdale	R2	254	42	58	0	....	1	1	1
Ajax	R3	550	39	58	15	3.3	(1 disc.)	0	2
Shopper's World	R4	177	37	54	0	....	1	1	1
Thorncliffe	R5	138	32	38	9	2.6	(1 disc.)	1	1
Cedarbrae	R6	278	30	41	9	....	1	2	2
Dixie	R7	401	29	40	11	....	(1 disc.)	2	2
Lawrence	R8	210	23	36	7	2.7	1	2	1
Northtown	S1	200	34	47	8	....	0	3	1
Knob Hill	S2	287	32	46	6	....	0	0	0
Dufferin	S3	23	32	45	3	6.3	0	2	2
Crang	S4	217	32	44	11	2.2	0	0	1
Richmond Heights	S5	502	32	39	0	2.5	0	1	1
Golden Mile	S6	165	31	43	14	....	0	2	2
Applewood	S7	401	31	34	16	8.1	0	1	2
Parkway	S8	162	26	36	15	2.7	0	2	1

TABLE 23--Continued

PLANNED CENTRES

Name	No.	Census Tract	Ground Floor Business Types	Number of Establishments		Per Cent Vacant	Number of Department Stores	Number of Chain Variety Stores	Number of Supermarkets
				Ground	Upper				
Rexdale	S9	273	26	35	9	....	0	1	1
Royal York	S10	269	26	30	10	3.2	0	1	1
Eglinton	S11	166	22	26	4	....	1	1	1
Bayview V.	C1	193	30	40	8	16.7	0	0	1
Humbertown	C2	301	28	38	0	....	0	0	1
North Park	C3	224	27	33	0	....	0	1	1
White Shield	C4	163	25	30	8	3.8	0	1	1
Jane Park	C5	242	23	23	4	14.8	0	1	1
Stonegate	C6	249	23	23	0	....	0	1	1
Sheppard	C7	211	22	30	9	8.3	0	1	1
Eastown	C8	286	22	29	13	....	0	1	1
Newtonbrook	C9	201	22	26	3	2.1	0	1	1
Westown	C10	269	20	21	7	4.7	0	0	2
Kipling Heights	C11	272	19	19	0	....	0	0	1
Cedar Heights	C12	280	18	22	12	5.2	0	1	1
Downsview	C13	294	17	21	3	5.5	0	1	2
Sunnybrook	C14	136	17	20	2	5.5	0	1	1
York Plaza	C15	217	13	15	4	6.6	0	1	1

TABLE 23--Continued

Cliffside	C16	172	13	15	4	....	0	1	2
Markham	C17	513	13	13	3	....	0	1	1
6 Points	C18	254	12	12	3	7.6	0	1	1
Albion Hall	C19	274	10	10	2	....	0	0	1
York Mills	N1	197	17	19	0	5.5	0	0	1
Hillside	N2	168	17	21	5	5.5	0	0	1
Westway	N3	270	18	18	8	....	0	0	1
Winston	N4	219	19	21	1	5.0	0	0	1
Eglinton Kenn.	N5	167	19	22	8	9.5	0	0	0
Kenlington	N6	285	19	26	22	5.0	0	0	0
Kennedy Park	N7	167	19	20	5	5.0	0	0	1
Bathurst	N8	293	18	19	9	....	0	0	1
Parkwoods	N9	192	17	19	0	....	0	0	1
The Hub	N10	168	17	18	8	....	0	0	1
Wexford Heights	N11	283	17	18	0	5.5	0	0	1
Donwood S.C.	N12	192	17	17	0	5.5	0	0	1
Bayview Mall	N13	193	11	12	0	....	0	0	1
Alderwood	N14	252	16	17	2	5.8	0	0	1
Bayview Plaza	N15	501	16	17	0	15.8	0	0	1
Orton Parkway	N16	280	16	17	1	5.8	0	0	1
Dixieland S.C.	N17	165	16	17	0	....	0	0	1
Finch-Main	N18	215	16	17	0	....	0	0	1

TABLE 23--Continued

PLANNED CENTRES

Name	No.	Census Tract	Ground Floor Business Types	Number of Establishments		Per Cent Vacant	Number of Department Stores	Number of Chain Variety Stores	Number of Supermarkets
				Ground	Upper				
Willowdale	N19	199	16	17	0	5.8	0	0	1
Thistletown	N20	274	16	16	6	....	0	0	1
Skyline	N21	283	15	19	2	6.2	0	0	1
Thorncrest	N22	266	15	15	4	....	0	0	1
Allencourt	N23	502	15	15	0	....	0	0	1
Cliffcrest	N24	170	14	18	0	....	0	0	1
Sheppard-Keele	N25	218	14	16	3	....	0	0	1
Elane	N26	168	14	15	0	5.5	0	0	1
Finchurst	N27	203	14	14	11	6.6	(1 disc.)	0	1
Ridgemoor	N28	172	14	14	2	6.6	0	0	1
East Mall	N29	265	14	14	0	....	0	0	1
Princess	N30	190	13	19	9	....	0	0	1
Tremingdon	N31	189	13	18	0	13.3	0	0	1
West Rouge	N32	551	13	14	0	13.3	0	0	1
Guildwood Village	N33	169	13	13	0	18.7	0	0	1
Streetsville	N34	407	13	13	0	18.7	0	0	1
Lorne Park S.C.	N35	403	13	13	0	....	0	0	1

TABLE 23--Continued

Glen Agar	N36	265	13	13	0	....	0	0	1
West Hill	N37	156	13	13	0	....	0	0	1
Kipling	N38	272	12	12	10	....	0	0	1
Lakeshore	N39	400	12	12	0	7.6	0	0	1
Birchmount	N40	289	12	12	0	....	0	0	1
Wishing Well	N41	161	11	11	2	....	0	0	1
Tom O'Shanter	N42	161	11	11	0	15.3	0	0	1
Elmhurst	N43	272	10	10	8	....	0	0	1
Dixie Belle	N44	405	10	10	7	16.6	0	0	1
Horton Building	N45	160	10	10	4	....	0	0	1
Park Royal	N46	403	10	10	0	23.0	0	1	1
Martin Grove	N47	270	9	9	5	....	0	0	1
Bendale	N48	279	9	9	7	....	0	0	1
Briarcrest	N49	271	8	8	4	....	0	0	1
Westmall Bloor	N59	271	8	8	1	....	0	0	1
Crestview	N60	402	5	5	10	2.85	0	0	1

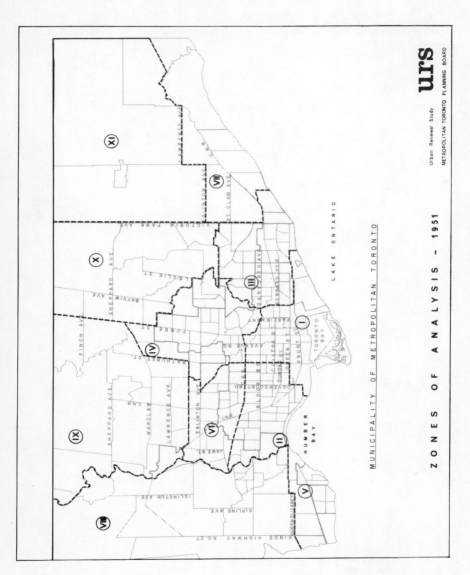

Fig. 23.--Zones of Analysis, 1951

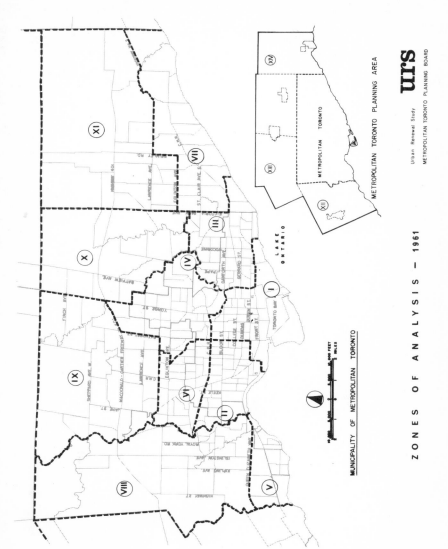

Fig. 24.--Zones of Analysis, 1961

APPENDIX C--ZONE DATA

TABLE 24

ZONE DATA--1951

Zone	Name	Population	Income[a]	Stores	Sales (000's)	Factor Scores[b]				
						I	II	III	IV	V
I	Central	121,301	2,284	2,233	138,391	0.23	0.99	0.88	-0.85	0.51
II	West End	230,209	2,513	3,466	182,462	0.34	0.42	1.08	0.27	-0.37
III	East End	235,554	2,635	2,850	188,510	1.26	0.37	-0.56	0.63	-0.70
IV	Uptown	175,839	3,601	1,767	147,242	-1.33	0.22	-0.25	0.06	-0.38
V	Lakeshore	42,356	2,788	528	38,141	0.52	-0.45	0.16	0.64	0.46
VI	Northwest	124,354	2,608	1,545	105,381	0.01	-0.21	0.33	0.47	-0.90
VII	Scarboro S.	35,746	2,681	256	17,592	0.65	-0.46	-0.67	0.33	1.52
VIII	Etobicoke	42,686	3,782	275	27,377	-0.70	-1.18	-0.29	0.26	0.27
IX	N. York	55,618	2,939	344	30,140	-0.04	-1.11	0.04	0.45	0.77
X	Bayview	20,221	3,371	137	11,730	-0.55	-0.82	-0.82	-0.92	0.55
XI	Scarboro N.	8,291	2,641	63	3,404	0.00	-0.96	0.01	-0.81	2.18

[a]Median earnings wage-earner family head.

[b]Zone factor score $= \sum_i p_i \, II_i \dfrac{1}{\sum p_i}$ where i identifies census tract.
p refers to population.
II identifies the factor.

TABLE 25

ZONE DATA--1961

Zone	Name	Population	Income[a]	Stores	Sales	Factor Scores						
						I	II	III	IV	V	VI	VII
I	Central	111,936	3,073	2,405	223,967	0.50	-0.50	-1.99	-0.37	-0.70	-0.25	0.46
II	West End	243,250	3,476	3,641	242,730	0.65	-0.40	-0.23	-0.68	0.29	1.41	0.23
III	East End	243,676	3,992	3,064	250,988	0.64	-0.71	0.33	0.74	0.62	-0.75	0.57
IV	Uptown	196,693	6,040	2,325	255,035	-1.27	-1.01	0.20	-0.42	0.22	-0.57	-0.13
V	Lakeshore	60,610	4,340	646	75,565	0.46	-0.11	0.39	0.77	-0.14	0.66	-0.46
VI	Northwest	153,814	3,608	1.789	141,780	1.05	-0.39	0.50	-0.65	0.32	-0.36	-0.69
VII	Scarboro S.	99,391	4,821	919	101,742	-0.08	1.05	-0.23	0.57	0.36	-0.09	-0.35
VIII	Etobicoke	138,060	6,201	1,069	150,796	-0.63	0.79	0.61	0.21	0.42	0.74	-0.27
IX	N. York	173,723	4,868	1,292	181,021	0.11	0.37	0.75	-0.72	-1.09	-0.28	-0.26
X	Bayview	80,924	6,611	452	81,964	-1.04	0.62	0.31	-0.24	-1.10	-0.47	0.17
XI	Scarboro N.	103,486	5,408	661	85,224	-0.14	1.05	0.43	0.90	-0.82	0.03	0.44
XII	Far West	74,875	5,390	803	81,480	-0.26	1.24	-0.06	0.33	-0.06	0.19	-0.25
XIII	Far North	56,370	3,951	657	56,948	-0.50	1.45	-0.62	0.49	0.75	-0.33	-0.62
XIV	Far East	30,955	3,776	243	15,851	0.06	1.87	-1.13	0.95	0.65	-0.11	-0.76

[a] Average earnings wage-earner family head.

111

TABLE 26

ZONE DATA--1951-1961

Zone	Name	Δ Population	ΔIncome[a]	Δ Stores	Δ Sales	$i_{population}$[b]	i_{income}	i_{stores}	i_{sales}
I	Central	- 9,365	789	162	30,383	- 0.8	3.0	0.7	4.9
II	West End	13,041	963	175	35,578	0.6	3.3	0.5	2.9
III	East End	8,122	1,357	214	45,030	0.4	4.5	0.7	2.9
IV	Uptown	20,854	2,439	558	72,501	1.1	5.3	2.6	5.6
V	Lakeshore	18,254	1,552	118	17,299	3.6	4.5	2.1	7.1
VI	Northwest	29,460	1,000	244	25,299	2.1	3.3	1.5	3.0
VII	Scarboro S.	63,645	2,140	663	74,835	10.8	6.0	13.7	19.2
VIII	Etobicoke	95,374	2,469	794	101,185	12.4	5.2	14.5	18.6
IX	N. York	118,105	1,929	948	130,798	12.1	5.2	14.1	19.7
X	Bayview	60,708	3,230	315	62,962	14.9	7.0	12.7	21.5
XI	Scarboro N.	95,195	2,767	598	70,549	28.7	9.4	26.5	16.6

[a]Income change distorted by change from median wage (1951) to average wage (1961).

[b]$\text{Log } (1 + i) = \dfrac{\log 1961 - \log 1951}{10}$

APPENDIX D--SPECIAL CENSUS ANALYSIS

SPECIAL CENSUS ANALYSIS

The results of the factor analysis of census material by Berry and
Murdie were an important source of information about consumer demand. Although
their study was focused on urban renewal and concentrated on the social factors
which imply residential problem areas, the description of the commercial structure required the use of all dimensions including ethnic patterns which are
unrelated to blight. It should also be noted that the results used in commercial study were drawn from an early stage of the census analysis so that there
are slight changes in the table of factor loadings presented here from those
found in the other report. These changes are trivial and do not affect the
interpretation.

1961 Census

The Dominion Bureau of Statistics Census Tract Bulletin CT-15, contains
181 measures of socio-economic characteristics for each census tract in the
census metropolitan area. After an initial selection procedure which eliminated
variables which were trivial, redundant, or presented measurement problems, 75
variables remained. These variables all shed some light on the pattern of
socio-economic variation in the city, yet many of them are highly interrelated,
and in terms of sheer number, they are difficult to handle.

A principal components factor analysis with varimax rotation derived
from these 75 variables seven orthogonal factors, which contained over 77 per
cent of the original variation. The output from the computer program includes
the factor loadings which relate the resultant factors to the input variables
(partially reproduced in Table 27) and the factor scores, measurements for each
census tract on these new variables. The factors may be identified by the factor loadings. Since each factor is independent of the others, the effect of
the factors may be considered as additive, i.e., each factor explains a certain
proportion of the total variable in turn, each pattern being superimposed on
the earlier ones.

Each factor has a different pattern of spatial variation.[1] Factor one,
labelled socio-economic rank because it includes income, education, and occu-
pation variables, defines a set of alternative upper and lower class sectors
around the downtown area. Factor two, family structure, varies in a series of
rings centred on the Yonge-St. Clair area. As one goes outward there is a

---

[1]See maps in Murdie and Berry.

regular increase in such variables as single family dwellings, family size, proportion of children, etc. A low score on factor three, household amenities, identifies the older areas of the city which are deficient in various living facilities. Four and six are ethnic factors which identify Jewish-Polish and Ukrainian-German areas respectively. The fifth factor, residential stability, exhibits a doughnut pattern with inner city and new suburban zones of high mobility. Factor seven, although not well defined, has some of the attributes of boarding house areas.

For the purpose of our analysis these factor scores were summarized for the zones of analysis defined in Chapter II. For instance, the value of factor II for zone 9 is $\sum_{i=1}^{n} P_i II_i / \sum_{i=1}^{n} P_i$ where n is the number of census tracts in zone 9, P_i and II_i are the population and factor score of the ith tract, respectively. The scores by zone are found in Appendix C.

1951 Census

Seventy-five operational variables were again selected from the 162 variables of the 1951 Census Tract Bulletin for Toronto, and the factor analysis produced five factors which explained 65 per cent of the original variation. The factor loadings are identified in Table 28. There are some interesting differences. The social rank and family structure factors remain almost unchanged, although the sign of the latter has been reversed during the rotation process. The ethnic variation is represented by only one factor, factor three, and the mobility and amenity measures are combined in one factor, five. The patterns of these variables are roughly similar to their counter parts described for 1961. Factor four, a strong factor in 1951 representing white-collar clerical workers, disappeared in the 1961 analysis.

Change, 1951-1961

As pointed out in the text, the metropolitan population has changed greatly during the decade 1951-1961. There are long-run continuing changes: increases in population, proportion non-British, income level, the possession of automobiles and appliances; and within the city there are short-run shifts in the spatial distributions as the various social areas expand or contract over time.

Some of the change is indicated by the results of the two factor analyses for 1951 and 1961. First, different factors emerge as the patterns of individual input variables have changed with respect to one another. Secondly, the spatial distribution of the factors is altered as income or ethnic groups move in or out of a given neighbourhood. Another noticeable difference in

TABLE 27

FACTOR LOADINGS--1961[1]

	Low Social Rank	Suburban Family	Many Household Amenities	Anglo-Saxon Protestant	Residential Stability	Central European	Boarding House
Per Cent of Total Variance	30.4	44.9	55.3	66.3	70.5	74.6	77.4
	I	II	III	IV	V	VI	VII
Population Under 15		.843					
Married			.723				
Born Outside Canada	.517	-.608					
British Isles				.762			
French			-.563				
German						.516	
Italian	.714						
Polish				-.585		.542	
Ukrainian						.812	
Other European				-.667			
Language Neither English nor French	.689						
Anglican				.646			
Jewish				-.769			
Roman Catholic	.716						
Greek Catholic						.762	
United Church	-.530			.597			
Not Attending School		-.870					
Elementary School Education	.840						
High School 1-2 years				.763			
3-5 years	-.919						
University	-.961						
6-9 Persons/House	.657						
Total Persons/House	.629	.546					
Lodgers	.517	-.571					
Persons/Family		.919					
Children/Family		.897					

TABLE 27--<u>Continued</u>

	Low Social Rank	Suburban Family	Many Household Amenities	Anglo-Saxon Protestant	Residential Stability	Central European	Boarding House
Per Cent of Total Variance	30.4	44.9	55.3	66.3	70.5	74.6	77.4
	I	II	III	IV	V	VI	VII
Wage Earners				.551			
Income/Family Head	-.686						
Single Detached Dwellings		.674					
Apartments		-.622					
Rooms/Dwelling							.589
Persons/Room	.791						
Owner-Occupied		.573	.508				
Median Value of Room	-.763						
Mortgaged		.519					
Occupied 1-2 Years					-.624		
Occupied 10 Years +					.802		
Furnace Heat			.524				
Flush Toilet			.700				
Bath			.704				
Refrigeration			.781				
Television			.767				
Automobile		.628	.524				
Females/Labor Force		-.833					
Unemployed Males	.628						
Self-Employed Males	-.680						
Self-Employed Females			-.512	-.507			
Managers (Male)	-.862						
Professional (Male)	-.916						
Clerical (Male)		-.629		.572			
Sales (Male)	-.751						
Service (Male)	.585						
Transport (Male)	.809						

TABLE 27--<u>Continued</u>

Per Cent of Total Variance	30.4	44.9	55.3	66.3	70.5	74.6	77.4
	I	II	III	IV	V	VI	VII
Craftsmen (Male)	.905						
Labourers (Male)	.886						
Managers (Female)	-.679						
Professional (Female)	-.875						
Clerical (Female)				.554	.530		
Sales (Female)					.558		
Service (Female)					-.529		
Craftsmen (Female)	.819						
Male Income 1000-1999	.571				-.525		
2000-2999	.726						
6000-9999	-.670						
10,000 +	-.878						
Average Earnings	-.774						
Female Income 1000-1999	.716						
2000-2999	.674						
6000 +	-.721						
Average Earnings	-.798						

[1]Murdie and Berry identified factor I as Economic Achievements, Factor II as Family Structure, Factor 3 as Household Characteristics and Factor V as Residential Stability.

TABLE 28

FACTOR LOADINGS--1951

INPUT VARIABLES	Low Socio-Economic Level	Urban Downtown	Non-British Origin	White Collar Workers	High-Mobility Low-Amenity Housing
	23.3	37.8	46.0	59.5	65.1
	I	II	III	IV	V
Sex Ratio	-.514				
Population Under 15		-.794			
Married		-.534			
British Isles			-.838		
Italian			.603		
Polish			.714		
Ukrainian			.745		
Other European			.662		
Asiatic		.514			
Language Neither English Nor French			.676		
Anglican			-.731		
Greek Orthodox			.634		
Jewish			.674		
Roman Catholic			.538		
Greek Catholic			.674		
United Church			-.603		
Not Attending School		.820			
Educated 1-4 years			.683		
5-8 years	.834				
9-12 years			-.511	.609	
13 years +	-.909				
6-9 Persons/House	.680				
Persons/House	.632				
Lodgers		.625	.531		
Children/Family		-.581			
Persons/Family		-.673			
Wage Earners	.567			.595	

TABLE 28--Continued

	23.3	37.8	46.0	59.5	65.1
	I	II	III	IV	V
Median Earnings	−.699				
Single Detached Dwellings		−.686			
Rooms/Dwelling					−.533
Persons/Room	.812				
Owner-Occupied		−.748			
Mortgaged		−.677			
Median Rent	−.678				
Occupied Pre-1946					−.598
1950-1951					.581
Furnace Heat					−.515
Flush Toilet					−.707
Bath					−.698
Refrigerators	−.794				
Automobile		−.651			
Females/Labor Force		.879			
Males Unemployed		.538			
Males Self-Employed	−.708				
Males Managers	−.883				
Professional	−.875				
Clerical				.689	
Manufacturing	.809				
Transport	.862				
Commerce	−.802				
Service	.657				
Labourers	.702				

TABLE 28--<u>Continued</u>

	Low Socio-Economic Level	Urban Downtown	Non-British Origin	White Collar Workers	High-Mobility Low-Amenity Housing
	23.3	37.8	46.0	59.5	65.1
	I	II	III	IV	V
Female Professional	-.658				
Clerical				.726	
Manufacturing	.742		.508		
Transport				.585	
Service				-.530	
Labourers	.524				
Male Earnings--1000		.549		-.539	
1000-1999	.542	.614			
4000 +	-.790				
Median Earnings	-.642				
Female Earnings--1000				-.681	
1000-1999	.668				
4000 +	-.679				
Median Earnings				.599	

patterns is due to the growth process. The 1951 maps show remnants of the old urban structure, the suburban towns and the transportation routes existing at an earlier time, in the form of sharp variations in social characteristics from tract to tract. By 1961 these have disappeared within Metro itself, creating broad homogeneous zones. The elements of the structure are now visible farther out where the old towns still remain distinct and readily identifiable.

The Enumeration Area Analysis

The final phase of the census analysis used as input is a series of tapes obtained from the Dominion Bureau of Statistics containing data on census variables by enumeration area, a smaller unit than the census tract, with 2,930 contained in the study area. Attention was focused on 46 measures of household characteristics. Although the results were not used directly as inputs to the commercial analysis, they have some relevance to the interpretation of our finding. In brief:

Factor 1--Apartments versus single family dwellings

Factor 2--Old, high density, single attached

Factor 3--Older, stable residential areas

Factor 4--Large, high value, high amenity homes

Factor 5--Older areas, lacking televisions, refrigerators; shared bath

Factor 6--Rent

Factor 7--Low value housing, in need of repair and lacking furnaces,
hot and cold water, and baths

Factor 8--New construction

Since these factors are all independent of one another it is important to note that there are three distinct blight factors (two, five, and seven) each with its own pattern of occurrence.

APPENDIX E--RESULTS FROM REGRESSIONS

TABLE 29

VARIABLES USED IN REGRESSION ANALYSIS

Symbol	Operating Definition
P^1	$\sum\limits_{Zone} P^i$ where P^i is the population of census tract i
I^1	$\sum\limits_{Zone} f_i i^i \Big/ \sum\limits_{Zone} f_i$ where f_i is the number of families with wage-earner family heads in census tract i
	i^i is the income of wage-earner family heads in census tract i (median in 1951, average in 1961)
E^2	$\sum\limits_{Zone} e_i$ where e_i is the number of retail and service establishments in census tract i
S^2	$\sum\limits_{Zone} S_i$ where S_i is the sales of retail and service establishments in census tract i
I, II, III, etc.	$= \sum\limits_{Zone} P_i II_i \Big/ \sum\limits_{Zone} P_i$ where II_i = factor score on Factor II for census tract i
Total Est.	= Total number of commercial establishments in zone identified in field study
Food Auto General Clothing Household Other Finance Community Services Business Services Personal Services Miscellaneous	Number of establishments of this business type in zone identified in field study (see Appendix A, Table 21).
Log Est.	$= \text{Log}_{10}$ (Total Establishments)
B.T.	= Number of business types as defined in Table 21
ΔE ΔS ΔP ΔI	Absolute difference in measure, 1951-1961
i_e i_s i_p i_i	Average annual per cent change in variable, 1951-1961. $= [\text{antilog } \dfrac{\text{Log}_{10} 1961 - \text{Log}_{10} 1951}{10} - 1] \times 100$

[1]Data derived from Dominion Bureau of Statistics, _Population and Housing Characteristics by Census Tracts_, Bulletin CT-6 (Ottawa, 1953); _Population and Housing Characteristics by Census Tracts_, Bulletin CT-15 (Ottawa, 1963).

[2]Data derived from Dominion Bureau of Statistics, _Selected Distribution Statistics by Census Tract for 14 Canadian Cities_ (Ottawa, 1954); _Retail Trade, Metropolitan Areas by Census Tracts_ and _Service Trade, Metropolitan Areas by Census Tracts_ (Ottawa, 1964).

TABLE 30

REGRESSION COEFFICIENTS--1961, THREE FACTORS

Dependent Variable		Independent Variables				R^2
		Population	I	II	III	
Total Stores	= 114.0 +	0.01283 (0.00096)	− 1.185 (0.647)	− 3.955 (0.690)	− 4.733 (0.590)	0.988
Food	= −77.2 +	0.00204 (0.00028)	+ 0.3495 (0.1885)	− 0.1412 (0.2010)	− 0.6242 (0.1717)	0.947
Automobile	= −14.7 +	0.00071 (0.00009)	+ 0.2776 (0.0613)	− 0.0396 (0.0654)	− 0.0934 (0.0559)	0.961
General	= 16.4 +	0.00090 (0.00023)	+ 0.0906 (0.1553)	+ 0.1242 (0.1656)	− 0.0725 (0.1415)	0.772
Clothing	= −26.8 +	0.00139 (0.00024)	+ 0.0293 (0.1607)	− 0.2470 (0.1714)	− 0.3615 (0.1464)	0.927
Household	= − 8.9 +	0.00095 (0.00011)	+ 0.0599 (0.0734)	− 0.1651 (0.0793)	− 0.3248 (0.0677)	0.966
Other	= 11.4 +	0.00145 (0.00016)	− 0.1779 (0.1061)	− 0.3361 (0.1132)	− 0.4000 (0.0967)	0.970
Finance	= 52.8 +	0.00063 (0.00030)	− 0.8237 (0.2107)	− 0.4905 (0.2151)	− 0.0360 (0.1838)	0.828
Community Services	= 102.6 +	0.00099 (0.00044)	− 0.2757 (0.2926)	− 0.9791 (0.3120)	− 1.2183 (0.2666)	0.878
Business Services	= 49.2 +	0.00025 (0.00028)	− 0.7391 (0.1859)	− 0.5688 (0.1982)	− 0.1746 (0.1694)	0.785
Personal Services	= 24.4 +	0.00326 (0.00026)	+ 0.2431 (0.1721)	− 0.8891 (0.1835)	− 1.1608 (0.1568)	0.987
Miscellaneous	= 20.9 +	0.00020 (0.00008)	− 0.1774 (0.0511)	− 0.2899 (0.0545)	− 0.2480 (0.0466)	0.933

TABLE 31

REGRESSION COEFFICIENTS--1961, SEVEN FACTORS

Dependent Variable	Population	Independent Variables							R^2
		I	II	III	IV	V	VI	VII	
Total Stores	0.0123 (.00215)	-1.376 (0.797)	-4.096 (0.808)	-4.673 (1.010)	-0.745 (1.662)	0.479 (1.628)	0.981 (0.792)	-.173 (2.640)	0.992
Food	0.00154 (.00052)	0.341 (0.192)	-0.160 (0.195)	-0.475 (0.244)	-0.436 (0.401)	0.330 (0.393)	0.377 (0.191)	0.518 (0.637)	0.988
Automobile	0.00046 (.00019)	0.299 (0.072)	-0.054 (0.073)	0.005 0.091	-0.118 (0.149)	0.217 (0.146)	0.030 (0.071)	0.346 (0.237)	0.978
General	0.00059 (.00056)	0.165 (0.206)	0.147 (0.209)	0.077 (0.261)	-0.263 (0.429)	0.378 (0.420)	-0.202 (0.204)	0.342 (0.681)	0.833
Clothing	0.00076 (0.00039)	0.052 (0.145)	-0.260 (0.147)	-0.148 (0.184)	-0.528 (0.302)	0.491 (0.296)	0.289 (0.144)	0.676 (0.480)	0.975
Household	0.00074 (0.00023)	0.056 (0.085)	-0.199 (0.086)	-0.246 (0.108)	-0.124 (0.177)	0.223 (0.174)	0.092 (0.085)	0.229 (0.282)	0.981
Other	0.00097 (0.00026)	-0.143 (0.097)	-0.356 (0.098)	-0.213 (0.123)	-0.379 (0.202)	0.489 (0.198)	0.063 (0.096)	0.494 (0.321)	0.990
Finance	0.00149 (0.00054)	-0.981 (0.202)	-0.561 (0.204)	-0.394 (0.255)	0.512 (0.420)	-0.541 (0.412)	-0.023 (0.200)	-1.472 (0.667)	0.929
Commercial Services	0.00122 (0.00090)	-0.216 (0.332)	-0.803 (0.337)	-1.328 (0.421)	-0.065 (0.692)	-0.600 (0.678)	0.038 (0.330)	-0.044 (1.099)	0.934
Business Services	0.00119 (0.00052)	-0.900 (0.193)	-0.637 (0.196)	-0.561 (0.245)	0.626 (0.403)	-0.657 (0.394)	-0.017 (0.192)	-1.468 (0.639)	0.904
Personal Services	0.00289 (0.00053)	0.204 (0.198)	-0.982 (0.201)	-1.041 (0.251)	-0.099 (0.413)	0.323 (0.404)	0.296 (0.197)	0.462 (0.655)	0.993
Miscellaneous	0.00035 (0.00019)	-0.206 0.072	-0.308 (0.073)	-0.308 (0.091)	0.115 (0.149)	-0.093 (0.146)	0.002 (0.071)	-0.225 0.237	0.945

THE UNIVERSITY OF CHICAGO
DEPARTMENT OF GEOGRAPHY
RESEARCH PAPERS (Planographed, 6 × 9 Inches)

(Available from Department of Geography, Rosenwald Hall, The University of Chicago, Chicago, Illinois, 60637. Price: four dollars each; by series subscription, three dollars each.)

*1. GROSS, HERBERT HENRY. *Educational Land Use in the River Forest–Oak Park Community* (*Illinois*)

*2. EISEN, EDNA E. *Educational Land Use in Lake County, Ohio*

*3. WEIGEND, GUIDO GUSTAV. *The Cultural Pattern of South Tyrol* (*Italy*)

*4. NELSON, HOWARD JOSEPH, *The Livelihood Structure of Des Moines, Iowa*

*5. MATTHEWS, JAMES SWINTON. *Expressions of Urbanism in the Sequent Occupance of Northeastern Ohio*

*6. GINSBURG, NORTON SYDNEY. *Japanese Prewar Trade and Shipping in the Oriental Triangle*

*7. KEMLER, JOHN H. *The Struggle for Wolfram in the Iberian Peninsula, June, 1942—June, 1944: A Study in Political and Economic Geography in Wartime*

*8. PHILBRICK, ALLEN K. *The Geography of Education in the Winnetka and Bridgeport Communities of Metropolitan Chicago*

*9. BRADLEY, VIRGINIA. *Functional Patterns in the Guadalupe Counties of the Edwards Plateau*

*10. HARRIS, CHAUNCY D., and FELLMANN, JEROME DONALD. *A Union List of Geographical Serials*

*11. DE MEIRLEIR, MARCEL J. *Manufactural Occupance in the West Central Area of Chicago*

*12. FELLMANN, JEROME DONALD. *Truck Transportation Patterns of Chicago*

*13. HOTCHKISS, WESLEY AKIN. *Areal Pattern of Religious Institutions in Cincinnati*

*14. HARPER, ROBERT ALEXANDER. *Recreational Occupance of the Moraine Lake Region of Northeastern Illinois and Southeastern Wisconsin*

*15. WHEELER, JESSE HARRISON, JR. *Land Use in Greenbrier County, West Virginia*

*16. MCGAUGH, MAURICE EDRON. *The Settlement of the Saginaw Basin*

*17. WATTERSON, ARTHUR WELDON. *Economy and Land Use Patterns of McLean County, Illinois*

*18. HORBALY, WILLIAM. *Agricultural Conditions in Czechoslovakia, 1950*

*19. GUEST, BUDDY ROSS. *Resource Use and Associated Problems in the Upper Cimarron Area*

*20. SORENSEN, CLARENCE WOODROW. *The Internal Structure of the Springfield, Illinois, Urbanized Area*

*21. MUNGER, EDWIN S. *Relational Patterns of Kampala, Uganda*

*22. KHALAF, JASSIM M. *The Water Resources of the Lower Colorado River Basin*

*23. GULICK, LUTHER H. *Rural Occupance in Utuado and Jayuya Municipios, Puerto Rico*

*24. TAAFFE, EDWARD JAMES. *The Air Passenger Hinterland of Chicago*

*25. KRAUSE, ANNEMARIE ELISABETH. *Mennonite Settlement in the Paraguayan Chaco*

*26. HAMMING, EDWARD. *The Port of Milwaukee*

*27. CRAMER, ROBERT ELI. *Manufacturing Structure of the Cicero District, Metropolitan Chicago*

*28. PIERSON, WILLIAM H. *The Geography of the Bellingham Lowland, Washington*

*29. WHITE, GILBERT F. *Human Adjustment to Floods: A Geographical Approach to the Flood Problem in the United States*

30. OSBORN, DAVID G. *Geographical Features of the Automation of Industry*   1953. 120 pp.

*31. THOMAN, RICHARD S. *The Changing Occupance Pattern of the Tri-State Area, Missouri, Kansas, and Oklahoma*

*32. ERICKSEN, SHELDON D. *Occupance in the Upper Deschutes Basin, Oregon*

*33. KENYON, JAMES B. *The Industrialization of the Skokie Area*

*34. PHILLIPS, PAUL GROUNDS. *The Hashemite Kingdom of Jordan: Prolegomena to a Technical Assistance Program*

*35. CARMIN, ROBERT LEIGHTON. *Anápolis, Brazil: Regional Capital of an Agricultural Frontier*

36. GOLD, ROBERT N. *Manufacturing Structure and Pattern of the South Bend–Mishawaka Area*   1954. 224 pp. 6 folded inserts. 2 maps in pocket.

*37. SISCO, PAUL HARDEMAN. *The Retail Function of Memphis*

*38. VAN DONGEN, IRENE S. *The British East African Transport Complex*

*39. FRIEDMANN, JOHN R. P. *The Spatial Structure of Economic Development in the Tennessee Valley*

*40. GROTEWOLD, ANDREAS. *Regional Changes in Corn Production in the United States from 1909 to 1949*

*41. BJORKLUND, E. M. *Focus on Adelaide—Functional Organization of the Adelaide Region, Australia*

*42. FORD, ROBERT N. *A Resource Use Analysis and Evaluation of the Everglades Agricultural Area*

*43. CHRISTENSEN, DAVID E. *Rural Occupance in Transition: Sumter and Lee Counties, Georgia*

*44. GUZMÁN, LOUIS E. *Farming and Farmlands in Panama*

* Out of print.

*45. ZADROZNY, MITCHELL G. *Water Utilization in the Middle Mississippi Valley*

*46. AHMED, G. MUNIR. *Manufacturing Structure and Pattern of Waukegan–North Chicago*

47. RANDALL, DARRELL. *Factors of Economic Development and the Okovango Delta* 1956. 282 pp. (Research Paper No. 3, Program of Education and Research in Planning, The University of Chicago.)

48. BOXER, BARUCH. *Israeli Shipping and Foreign Trade* 1957. 176 pp.

49. MAYER, HAROLD M. *The Port of Chicago and the St. Lawrence Seaway* 1957. 283 pp.

50. PATTISON, WILLIAM D. *Beginnings of the American Rectangular Land Survey System, 1784–1800* 1957. 2d printing 1963. 260 pp.

*51. BROWN, ROBERT HAROLD. *Political Areal-Functional Organization: With Special Reference to St. Cloud, Minnesota*

*52. BEYER, JACQUELYN. *Integration of Grazing and Crop Agriculture: Resources Management Problems in the Uncompahgre Valley Irrigation Project*

53. ACKERMAN, EDWARD A. *Geography as a Fundamental Research Discipline* 1958. 40 pp. $1.00.

*54. AL-KHASHAB, WAFIQ HUSSAIN. *The Water Budget of the Tigris and Euphrates Basin*

55. LARIMORE, ANN EVANS. *The Alien Town: Patterns of Settlement in Busoga, Uganda* 1958. 210 pp.

56. MURPHY, FRANCIS C. *Regulating Flood-Plain Development* 1958. 216 pp.

*57. WHITE, GILBERT F., et al. *Changes in Urban Occupance of Flood Plains in the United States*

*58. COLBY, MARY MC RAE. *The Geographic Structure of Southeastern North Carolina*

*59. MEGEE, MARY CATHERINE. *Monterrey, Mexico: Internal Patterns and External Relations*

60. WEBER, DICKINSON. *A Comparison of Two Oil City Business Centers (Odessa-Midland, Texas)* 1958. 256 pp.

61. PLATT, ROBERT S. *Field Study in American Geography* 1959. 408 pp.

62. GINSBURG, NORTON, editor. *Essays on Geography and Economic Development* 1960. 196 pp.

63. HARRIS, CHAUNCY D., and FELLMANN, JEROME D. *International List of Geographical Serials* 1960. 247 pp.

64. TAAFFE, ROBERT N. *Rail Transportation and the Economic Development of Soviet Central Asia* 1960. 186 pp.

*65. SHEAFFER, JOHN R. *Flood Proofing: An Element in a Flood Damage Reduction Program*

66. RODGERS, ALLAN L. *The Industrial Geography of the Port of Genova* 1960. 150 pp.

67. KENYON, JAMES B. *Industrial Localization and Metropolitan Growth: The Paterson-Passaic District* 1960. 250 pp.

68. GINSBURG, NORTON. *An Atlas of Economic Development* 1961. 119 pp. 14 × 8½". Cloth $7.50. University of Chicago Press.

69. CHURCH, MARTHA. *Spatial Organization of Electric Power Territories in Massachusetts* 1960. 200 pp.

70. WHITE, GILBERT F., et al. *Papers on Flood Problems* 1961. 234 pp.

71. GILBERT, E. W. *The University Town in England and West Germany* 1961. 79 pp. 4 plates. 30 maps and diagrams.

72. BOXER, BARUCH. *Ocean Shipping in the Evolution of Hong Kong* 1961. 108 pp.

73. ROBINSON, IRA M. *New Industrial Towns on Canada's Resource Frontier* 1962. (Research Paper No. 4, Program of Education and Research in Planning, The University of Chicago.) 192 pp.

74. TROTTER, JOHN E. *State Park System in Illinois* 1962. 152 pp.

75. BURTON, IAN. *Types of Agricultural Occupance of Flood Plains in the United States* 1962. 167 pp.

76. PRED, ALLAN. *The External Relations of Cities During 'Industrial Revolution'* 1962. 124 pp.

77. BARROWS, HARLAN H. *Lectures on the Historical Geography of the United States as Given in 1933* Edited by WILLIAM A. KOELSCH. 1962. 248 pp.

78. KATES, ROBERT WILLIAM. *Hazard and Choice Perception in Flood Plain Management* 1962. 157 pp.

79. HUDSON, JAMES. *Irrigation Water Use in the Utah Valley, Utah* 1962. 249 pp.

80. ZELINSKY, WILBUR. *A Bibliographic Guide to Population Geography* 1962. 257 pp.

*81. DRAINE, EDWIN H. *Import Traffic of Chicago and Its Hinterland*

*82. KOLARS, JOHN F. *Tradition, Season, and Change in a Turkish Village*

83. WIKKRAMATILEKE, RUDOLPH. *Southeast Ceylon: Trends and Problems in Agricultural Settlement* 1963. 163 pp.

84. KANSKY, K. J. *Structure of Transportation Networks: Relationships between Network Geometry and Regional Characteristics* 1963. 155 pp.

85. BERRY, BRIAN J. L. *Commercial Structure and Commercial Blight* 1963. 254 pp.

86. BERRY, BRIAN J. L., and TENNANT, ROBERT J. *Chicago Commercial Reference Handbook* 1963. 278 pp.

87. BERRY, BRIAN J. L., and HANKINS, THOMAS D. *A Bibliographic Guide to the Economic Regions of the United States* 1963. 128 pp.

88. MARCUS, MELVIN G. *Climate-Glacier Studies in the Juneau Ice Field Region, Alaska* 1964. 128 pp

89. SMOLE, WILLIAM J. *Owner-Cultivatorship in Middle Chile* 1964. 176 pp.

90. HELVIG, MAGNE. *Chicago's External Truck Movements: Spatial Interaction between the Chicago Area and Its Hinterland* 1964. 132 pp.

* Out of print.

91. HILL, A. DAVID. *The Changing Landscape of a Mexican Municipio, Villa Las Rosas, Chiapas*
NAS-NRC Foreign Field Research Program Report No. 26. 1964. 121 pp.

92. SIMMONS, JAMES W. *The Changing Pattern of Retail Location* 1964. 212 pp.

93. WHITE, GILBERT F. *Choice of Adjustment to Floods* 1964. 164 pp.

94. MCMANIS, DOUGLAS R. *The Initial Evaluation and Utilization of the Illinois Prairies, 1815–1840* 1964. 109 pp.

95. PERLE, EUGENE D. *The Demand for Transportation: Regional and Commodity Studies in the United States* 1964. 130 pp.

96. HARRIS, CHAUNCY D. *Annotated World List of Selected Current Geographical Serials in English* 1964. 32 pp. $1.00

97. BOWDEN, LEONARD W. *Diffusion of the Decision To Irrigate: Simulation of the Spread of a New Resource Management Practice in the Colorado Northern High Plains* 1965. 146 pp.

98. KATES, ROBERT W. *Industrial Flood Losses: Damage Estimation in the Lehigh Valley* 1965. 76 pp.

99. RODER, WOLF. *The Sabi Valley Irrigation Projects* 1965. 213 pp.

100. SEWELL, W. R. DERRICK. *Water Management and Floods in the Fraser River Basin* 1965. 163 pp.

101. RAY, D. MICHAEL. *Market Potential and Economic Shadow: A Quantitative Analysis of Industrial Location in Southern Ontario* 1965. 164 pp.

102. AHMAD, QAZI. *Indian Cities: Characteristics and Correlates* 1965. 184 pp.

103. BARNUM, H. GARDINER. *Market Centers and Hinterlands in Baden-Württemberg*
NAS–NRC Foreign Field Research Report No. 27. 1966. 173 pp.

104. SIMMONS, JAMES W. *Toronto's Changing Retail Complex* 1966 126 pp.

105. SEWELL, W. R. DERRICK, *et al. Human Dimensions of Weather Modification* 1966. 423 pp.